Saint Luke of Simferopol

Spirit, Soul, Body

Gozalov Books
The Hague

This book has the blessing of
His Eminence Simon, Archbishop of Brussels and Belgium
and temporarily of The Hague and the Netherlands

ISBN: 9789079889648;978-90-79889-64-8
Second edition

Original title: «Дух, душа и тело»

Editor: Convent of the Mother of God Portaïtissa, Trazegnies, Belgium, portaitissa@skynet.be
Translators: Rimma Andronova and Guram Kochi MSc
Design: Guram Kochi MSc and Marijcke Tooneman
Front cover: photo of St. Luke
The Scriptural quotes are taken from the The Sacred Bible, Catholic Public Domain Version with thanks to the http://www.sacredbible.org/catholic/index.htm

© Gozalov Books, The Hague, 2014
Tel.: 00 31 (0) 70 352 15 65
E-mail: gozalovbooks@planet.nl
Website: www.hetsmallepad.nl

All rights reserved. No part of this publication may be reproduced or transmitted in any form or by any means, electronic or mechanical, including photocopy and recording, or stored in a retrieval system, without the written permission of the publisher.

Table of Contents

Introduction 5

Chapter 1. What Conclusions can we draw
              with regard to the existing System of Science 8
Chapter 2. The Heart as Organ of Cognition
              of the Highest 17
Chapter 3. The Brain and the Spirit. The Spirit in Nature 39
Chapter 4. The Spirit of Plants and Animals 54
Chapter 5. The Soul of Animal and the Soul of Man 60
Chapter 6. The Spirit is not indubitably connected
              with the Body and the Soul 73
Chapter 7. Transcendental spiritual Abilities 86
Chapter 8. On the inner Man 102
Chapter 9. Immortality 111

Introduction

The author of this book, Saint Luke the Confessor (secular name Valentine Voino-Jasenetsky) of Simferopol and Crimea was born on 27th April 1877 in Kertch, Crimea and he passed away to rest in Christ on 11th June 1961 in Simferopol, Crimea.

He was the descendant of a White-Russian-Polish impoverished princely line. By the end of his life he was an archbishop of the Russian Orthodox Church and at the same time a prominent physician, surgeon, scientist-researcher, inventor, author of scientific and theological works and painter.

From a young age his ideal was serving the weak and the sick. Therefore he ended his promising studies at the Academy of Fine Arts in Kiev unfinished and he started medical studies at Kiev University where he graduated. He chose to work in the province to help relieve the suffering of ordinary people. At the same time he did scientific research work on the cases of his practice and he learned several European languages in order to follow the development of medical science in the West. His innovative ideas and advanced surgery techniques have received broad acknowledgement in the Russian as well as in the European medical world.

He inherited a deep faith from his father and from his student years on he was known for his spontaneous public speeches on Christian ways and values.

At the time of the civil war after the Bolshevik revolution in Russia, when their consistent morbid and deadly persecution of the clergy was at full swing, Valentine Voino-Jasenetsky consented to be ordained as priest, and later he took monastic vows with the name Luke (after the Apostle and Evangelist Luke) and he was ordained as bishop. Being an intelligent and powerful spiritual pastor he was persecuted by the Soviet authorities. They convicted him on the base of false accusations and sentenced him to banishment in Siberia, above the Polar Circle, for nearly eleven years.

He ended his days as archbishop of Simferopol and Crimea. During all his ordeals he remained faithful to his Russian-Orthodox faith and his principles and he set forth his work as surgeon, physician and scientist, notwithstanding even blindness which struck him in the last decennium of his life.

We offer here a translation of his beautiful treaty on God, man and the universe, based on the Holy Scriptures, his religious experience and the works of scientists, theologians and philosophers.

The reader will even find clues with regard to the secrets of life in the whole universe, on the distant stars and planets that God's Spirit has revealed to Saint Luke.

The publisher
August 2014

Saint Luke the Confessor
of Simferopol and Crimea

"For the Word of God is living and effective: more piercing than any two-edged sword, reaching to the division even between the soul and the spirit, even between the joints and the marrow, and so it discerns the thoughts and intentions of the heart." (Hebr. 4:12)

"And may the God of peace himself sanctify you through all things, so that your whole spirit and soul and body may be preserved without blame unto the return of our Lord Jesus Christ." (1 Thess. 5:23)

Chapter 1. What Conclusions can we draw with regard to the existing System of Science

We are going to start our discourse on the interrelation of the human body, soul and spirit from a long time ago. Up to the end of the XIXth century, exact sciences impressed by the explicitness and precision of their treaties. Not long ago the main scientific postulates were taken as unconditionally true. Only a select few could see cracks in the colossal construction of classical science. The great scientific discoveries at the end of the previous and the beginning of this century however suddenly shook the foundations of this construction and forced us to review the main concepts of physics and mechanics. The principles, that seemed to have the most reliable mathematical framework, are being debated by scientists. Every page of such books as the profound work "The Science and the Hypotheses" by Henri Poincaré contains evidence of it. This famous mathematician has shown that even mathematics is based on plenty of hypotheses and conventions. One of his most outstanding colleagues-mathematicians, Emile Picker, in one of his works shows how incoherent are the principles of classical mechanics, the basic science which claims to have formulated the general laws of the universe. Ernst Mach in his "The History of Mechanics" expresses a similar viewpoint: "The foundations of mechanics, seemingly the most simple, are extremely complicated in fact; based on unrealized or even unrealizable experiments, they cannot be taken for the axioms of the mathematics."

The physicist Lucien Poincaré writes: "There are no longer great theories, which would [nowadays] enjoy a unanimous acceptance by the researchers; there is an evident anarchy in the field of science, none of its laws are accepted as truly necessary. We witness the breaking of old concepts, and not the completion of scientific works.

The ideas that seemed best well-founded to our predecessors are being revised. The possibility of explaining all phenomena on the grounds of mechanics is abandoned now. The very foundations of mechanics are disputed; new facts are shaking the absolute meaning of the laws considered to be the main ones."

However, though speaking of physics and mechanics 30-40 years ago it was possible to qualify them as being in a state of anarchy, this is no longer true. Breaking the main principles and concepts of physics has lead to the creation of new concepts, much more correct and profound. Not only those concepts over-rule old classical mechanics but they include it as an approximately valid theory with well-defined limits of applicability.

For example, it is found that classical mechanics cease to be valid for the smallest known objects, molecules, atoms, electrons etc. and must be replaced by a more precise and at the same time more complicated and abstract theory – quantum mechanics. And quantum mechanics is not something completely contrary to classical mechanics but it includes it as a kind of approximation which can be applied to massive objects.

Moreover, the processes characterized by high velocity movement, approaching the speed of light, can't be truly described with classical mechanics but must be replaced by the more rigorous theory of relativistic mechanics based on Einstein's relativity theory.

The law of the invariability of elements is no longer valid, because the transformation of one element into another is indisputably proved.

The established fact is the existence of elements with the same atomic weights but not identical chemical properties. A similar statement could have caused derision among chemists a few years ago (T. Svedberg).

There is hope for the complex structure of an atom to be proved, so there is no reasonable doubt in the possibility of heavy atoms being composed of lighter ones. In the last analysis all elements might be composed of hydrogen atoms. According to these hypotheses a helium atom comprises four hydrogen atoms closely spaced. In its turn, a hydrogen atom consists of two particles: an electron and a proton.

An atom is no longer the primary unit of matter, as it was set out that an atom is complex. Now the smallest known particles of matter are an electron and a positron. Both have the same mass but differ in their electric charge: an electron is negatively charged while the charge of a positron is positive.

In addition there are heavier particles, protons and neutrons, comprised in a nucleus. The mass of such a particle, 1840 times the mass of an electron, is almost equal; while a proton is positively charged, a neutron is electrically neutral.

It was recently found that cosmic rays coming inside the earth atmosphere from the interstellar space include a series of unknown particles, and their mass varies in a very large range (from 100 to 30 000 times more than an electron mass). These particles have got different names: mesons, or mesotrons, varytrons and others. It was also found that all these particles are not absolutely invariable. Protons may be changed into neutrons and vice versa, electrons in a composition with positrons may cease to exist as particles converting into radiation. On the other hand, under certain conditions an electromagnetic field may "give birth" to the pair, an electron and a positron. The particles found in cosmic rays may significantly alter their mass in the process of interaction with the atoms in the atmosphere.

Modern books on physics call "annihilation" (the destruction of matter) the process of conversion of an electron – positron pair into radiation, and the process in the opposite direction is called "materialization".

Consistent materialists call such terminology just conditionally acceptable, leading to idealistic distortions in the description of reality. They say there is no conversion of mass into energy and vice versa, because both mass and energy are properties of the particular reality called matter, and appearing particles are endowed with energy while energy is endowed with mass.

This last statement for us, brought up on the previous concepts of physics, is absolutely new, though we are very far from celebrating the victory over materialism.

We have neither the right nor the intention to deprecate the very important achievements of modern physics. The fact that particles may change their mass, like the new particles found in cosmic rays, or annihilate themselves converting into an electromagnetic field, like electrons and positrons, may not lead to the conclusion that matter disappears, as the electromagnetic field may be considered as the other form of matter.

Both these forms may be converted into one another the same way as liquids may change their form to solid or gas. These transformations though, are possible on condition that energy is constant according to the law. Energy cannot disappear or be created out of nothing. Only the form of the matter containing the energy may be changed, but the total amount of energy must be constant.

At present physicists reject the hypothesis of an existing weightless and "absolutely elastic" substance, the ether, replacing it with the concept of the electromagnetic field. The electromagnetic field is not a substance in the usual mechanical sense of the word, as it has no weight, it is not hard or elastic in a normal sense, it does not consist of particles, etc. But it is endowed with energy, so in this sense it should be considered as a form of existence of matter. It is generated by movements and interactions of elementary particles, electrons and others. On the other hand, the electromagnetic field itself acts on the particles and may even give rise to them under certain conditions.

Instead of weight, hardness, elasticity etc. the electromagnetic field has other characteristics that determine its properties. These characteristics are the intensity and direction of electric and magnetic forces in different points of the space.

The laws describing the electromagnetic field and its interaction with an electric charge are the subject of a particular field of physics – electrodynamics, and the laws of motion and interaction of material particles comprise a part of mechanics.

All products of matter dissociation are finally "absorbed" into electromagnetic fields. Regardless of the kind of dissociating matter and of the dissociation methods, the products of the dissociation are always the same. In case of nucleus disintegration of radioactive elements, of emission out of a metal surface under light, of interaction products in chemical or burning processes, the result is always the same with variety in quality, amount or speed. The matter disintegrates into elementary particles: neutrons, protons, mesons, electrons, positrons etc. The motion and interaction of these particles generate the electromagnetic field, magnetic and electric oscillations of different frequency, radio-waves, infra-red rays, visible radiation, ultra-violet and gamma-rays.

Electrical phenomena underlie all chemical reactions, and there is an attempt to explain all the other forces on their basis. It is found that light is also a form of electromagnetic energy, and electricity has the corpuscular, or as some wrongly name it, atomic structure. It is certainly not right to call atoms, the corpuscles forming electricity, electrons. Electricity is carefully and completely acceptably determined by Milliken. He says: "I have never tried to answer the question what electricity is; I am satisfied with the established fact that whatever it is by its nature, its amount will always be an exact multiple of a definite electrical unit.

...Electricity is something more fundamental than atoms of matter, because it is a substantial composition of hundreds of different particles. Like matter, it is something consisting of separate units, but it is different from those of matter, because all these units, as far as it could be defined, are absolutely equal."

The corpuscular theory of electricity is the greatest achievement of theoretical physics. However it can't be said that according to its corpuscular nature electricity ceases to be energy, and becomes something like matter. Physicists don't say so either, they just claim that energy has a certain mass, and "mass" is an immanent feature of some reality: matter. This is not an attempt to consider matter and energy as being the same; regardless of how close electricity is by its nature to matter, it remains energy for us, and the most important, the main part of atomic energy.

And yet this basis of the physical life of the world has become known to us only 300 years ago, from the time of Volta. For thousands of years electricity was unknown to people.

Only 50 years ago science was enriched by the knowledge of new and extremely important forms of energy - radio-waves, infra-red rays, cathode rays, radioactivity, and nuclear energy. The latter (we can't even imagine how grand and powerful it is) underlying the whole dynamics of the world, giving birth to unfading inexhaustible thermal energy from the sun, was discovered 300 years later than electricity.

Do we have the right to believe and even say that in the universe there are still other, unknown forms of energy, even more important to the world than nuclear energy?

34 % of the solar spectrum is invisible. Only a very small segment of those 34%, ultraviolet and infra-red rays, are studied, and the forms that underlie them are described now. And are there any reasonable arguments against the idea, even the certainty, that the numerous Fraunhofer lines hide many secrets, forms of energy unknown to us, maybe even more delicate than nuclear energy?

From a materialistic point of view these still unknown forms of energy should be some special forms of existence of matter.

Let it be so, we can say nothing in argument, believing in the power of science. However electricity cannot be called matter, and most certainly should be considered as energy; this energy can generate particles of matter having a definite mass and physical properties. These particles can annihilate that is turn into energy again. Following the logic of these facts we can assume that in future new forms of existence of matter (or rather, energy), will be discovered which according to their properties, may be called "semi-material" even more than is done for electricity.

The very concept of "semi-material" includes the recognition of the existence of "non-material".

Is there any reason to deny the legitimacy of our faith and confidence in the existence of a purely spiritual energy, or power, which we believe to be the primary source of all physical forms of energy, and through it the source of matter itself? What is our idea of this spiritual energy?

For us it is God's almighty love. Love may not exist for itself only, for its immanent feature is the need to pour out over somebody or something, and because of this need God has created the Universe.

"By the word of the Lord were the heavens made; and all the host of them by the breath of his mouth." (Psalm 32: 6).

This energy of love, which outpoured according to the will of the most good God: God's Word, gave rise to all the other forms of energy, which in turn generated particles of matter, and then, with their help - to the entire material world.

Pouring in other directions, God's manifested love created the entire spiritual world too: the world of angelic creatures gifted with reason, of human understanding and the entire world of pneumatic and psychic phenomena (Ps. 104:4; 32:6). The fact that we know nothing about many doubtlessly existing forms of energy, is due to the obvious lack of sensitivity of our poor five senses for discovering the world, and to the lack of new scientific methods and reagents for the detection of those forms which are not available to our senses.

But is it true that we have only five senses and no other organs and means of direct perception? Is there any possibility of a better perception of selected forms of energy adequate to them? The eagle's visual acuity, and the dog's sense of smell excel to a great extent that of humans. Pigeons are endowed with a sense of direction, which is beyond our comprehension, infallibly guiding them in their flight. The growing acuity of hearing and sense of touch of the blind is well known too.

I believe that the certainties of mental order, which will be described further on, not only oblige us to admit the possibility of a heightened sensitivity of our five senses, but also to add our heart to them as a special organ of sense: the seat of emotions and the organ of our cognition.

Chapter 2. The Heart as Organ of Cognition of the Highest

Already in the time of the ancient Greeks the word "heart" meant not only a carnal organ, but also the human's soul, mood, view, thought, even prudence, intelligence, conviction , etc. "Folk wisdom" gave a right value to the heart in human life already long before: "My heart stops beating – my life is over". That's why people call the heart "the engine of life". We know now quite well that the physical and spiritual well-being depends to a great extent on a proper function of the heart.

In our everyday life we may see that somebody's heart is suffering, aches, etc. It is possible to find expressions in literature and lyrics like: "My heart longs for... is happy...is feeling something" etc. Thus, the heart is like a sensory organ and, moreover, an extremely precise and versatile one. We should dwell upon this because all these phenomena have a profound physiological basis, described by I. P. Pavlov [a famous Russian physiologist]. In distant times, when our ancestors were in the zoological stage of development, they responded to all the stimuli they were receiving almost predominantly by muscular activity, which prevailed over all other instinctive acts. The entire muscular activity is in its turn closely connected to the cardiovascular activity.

Though the muscular reflexes of the modern civilized human being are reduced almost to a minimum level, the changes of the heart's activity, induced by them, have remained fully present.

The modern civilized man is accustomed to hiding his muscular reflexes, by working on himself. Only variations in his heart's activity may make his feelings evident. Thus, the heart still is an organ of feeling, precisely indicating our subjective state and always exposing it.

Being a doctor I should remark that as well-regulated as the cardio – activity is, caused by muscular activity, not excessive, of course, as badly-regulated is the cardio – activity caused by various emotions, which are not necessarily expressed in muscular activity. That is why the hearts of people in the learned professions, who perform just an easy manual labour, but who are excessively subjected to experiencing life's agitation, are affected much more.

Thus is a judgement on the functioning of the heart, of a pathologist-anatomist ("On the death of a man") and a great physiologist, Academician Ivan Pavlov, ("Course of Physiology," edited by Prof. Savich, 1924).

Moreover, the innervation of the heart is stunningly rich and complex; the heart is covered with a network of fibres of the sympathetic nervous system and through it, is very closely connected with the brain and spinal cord. The heart is provided with a complex system of cerebral fibres, which transmits a great number of highly complex impulses of the central nervous system from the vagus. It is quite possible that the centripetal sensory impulses of the heart are sent back to the brain through that very nervous system.

The functions of the sympathetic and vegetative nervous system are poorly studied and are almost unknown, but it is quite clear now that these functions are very important and versatile. And the most substantial thing for us is that these nerve fibres and nodes certainly play a very significant role in the physiology of sensitivity. Thus, our knowledge of the anatomy and physiology of the heart not only do not hinder but rather prompt us to consider the heart as being the most important sensory organ, not just the central pump of the blood circulation.

The Scriptures, however, tell us much more about the heart. Almost every page of the Bible refers to the heart, and those reading it for the first time can't help noticing that the heart is considered not only as the central organ of sense, but also as the most important organ of cognition, reflection and receptacle of the spiritual impulses. Moreover, according to the Scriptures the heart is man's organ of communication with God, and therefore, the organ of cognition of the Highest.

Truly all-embracing is the role of the heart in the realm of feelings according to the Scriptures. The heart feels joy (Jer.15:16); "delight" (Prov. 27:9), "afflicted" (Jer.4:19), "inflamed" to such an extent that the Psalmist is crying (Ps. 72(73):21), is "wounded" from malice (Acts 7:54), is "burning " with a trembling anticipation in Cleopas (Luke, 24:32), "seethes against God" (Prov. 19:3), is "filled with malice" (Eccles. 9:3), "adultery" (Matt. 5:28), "bitter zeal" (Jac. 3:14), arrogance (Prov. 16:5), courage (Ps. 26(27):3), "terror" (Lev. 26:36); "desire for impurity" (Rom. 1:24), "reproach" breaks it (Ps. 68(69): 20).

However it also perceives consolation, sense and comfort (Philem. 7), capable of a great feeling of trust in God (Ps. 26(27):7) and be broken to be near the Lord (Ps. (33)34:18); it may be a repository of meekness and lowliness (Matt. 11:29).

Besides the wide range of emotions and feelings, the heart has the higher ability of feeling God, about which Paul the Apostle says in the Areopagus of Athens: "so as to seek God, if perhaps they may consider him or find him..." (Acts 17:27) Many pious ascetics and reverend fathers tell about feeling the Lord or about gracious influences of the Spirit of God on the heart. All of them could feel to a greater or lesser extent the same as the Jewish prophet Jeremiah: "... my heart became like a raging fire, enclosed within my bones."(Jer. 20:9)

Where does this fire come from? St. Ephraim the Syrian, the great repository of the Divine Grace, gives us the answer: " Incomprehensible to the mind, It comes into the heart and dwells in it, thus the Innermost of the Radiance is to be found in the heart. The Earth exalts His feet, and the pure heart bears Him inside"; and, we may add, the heart contemplates Him without the eyes according to the Lord's word:
"Blessed are the pure in heart, for they shall see God."(Matt. 5:8). We may find a similar discourse by John Climacus: "the fire of the Holy Spirit coming into the heart revives the prayer; after the prayer has been revived and ascended to the Heavens, the descent of the heavenly fire into the chamber of the heart can take place. "

And these are the words of Macarius the Great: "The heart governs all the body's organs and, when the [God's] Grace would fill all parts of the heart, it dominates all man's thoughts and all the parts of his body for the mind and the soul's designs are there...For it is there we should look whether the grace of the law of the Spirit is written there."

What do we mean by "there"? We mean the main organ, where the throne of grace is, and the mind and the soul and all the soul's designs dwell, i.e. the heart.

Let us not cite too much from the works of those who lead the deepest spiritual life. Many can be found in "The Philokalia". All the holy Fathers say that, according to their own experience, when in a good and graceful state of soul they feel in their heart a quiet joy, deep inner peace and warmth in the heart, which always grow stronger after a steadfast and fervent prayer or good deeds. On the contrary, the influence of the spirit of Satan and his servants on the heart raises there a troubled uneasiness, a kind of burning pain, coldness and an unaccountable anxiety. These are the feelings in the heart according to which the ascetics recommend to assess one's spiritual state and to distinguish between the Spirit of Light and the spirit of darkness.

However the ability of the heart to communicate with God is not limited to this kind of more or less vague feelings. No matter how doubtful it may seem to unbelievers, we state that the heart is able to perceive certain suggestions directly as God's words. Moreover, this ability doesn't belong to the domain of saints solely. Even I, like many others, experienced it more than once with a tremendous power and deep emotion. While reading or listening to the Scriptures I sometimes suddenly was stunned realizing that God's words were addressed directly to me. They sounded to me like a thunderbolt, and pierced my brain and heart like lightning. Certain phrases, quite unexpectedly for me, just stood out from the context of the Scriptures, in a bright dazzling light and were indelibly imprinted in my mind. And these lightning phrases of God's words were always suggestions, instructions or even prophecies, most important and necessary for me at that moment and consistently proving true in the future.

Their strength was sometimes colossal, stunning, and incomparable with the power of any kind of common mental influences.

In part due to circumstances beyond my control I left my Episcopal ministry for a few years, but once during the all-night vigil service, waiting for the Gospel reading, I suddenly felt a shiver, a vague foreboding that something terrible was about to happen. These were words which I myself had often read calmly, "Simon, son of John, do you love me more than these? ... Feed my lambs." (John 21:15) I was shaken so suddenly and vigorously by God's reproach, His call for the resumption of the deserted service, that till the end of the vigil I was shivering all over, couldn't sleep the next night and for approximately a month and a half was shaken with sobs and tears each time I recalled this extraordinary event.

Let sceptics not think that this feeling was an impact of my own dreary memories of the sacred ministry I had deserted and reproaches of my conscience. On the contrary, I was focused at that time on my illness and the impending surgery, and I was in the most ordinary state of mind, very far from any exaltation.

The holy prophets could listen directly to God's words and take them into their hearts. " And he said to me: "Son of man, listen with your ears, and take into your heart, all my words, which I am speaking to you." (Ezek. 3:10)

"My heart has spoken to you; my face has sought you. I yearn for your face, O Lord." (Ps. 26(27):8)

The prophet Jeremiah qualifies the call from above as God's direct speaking to him.

The prophet Ezekiel, having described his marvellous vision of God's glory, continues: "This was the vision of the likeness of the glory of the Lord. And I saw, and I fell on my face, and I heard the voice of someone speaking. And he said to me: "Son of man, stand on your feet, and I will speak with you. And after this was spoken to me, the Spirit entered into me, and he set me on my feet. And I heard him speaking to me," (Ezek. 1:28- 2:2)

All the prophets speak in the name of God: "And The Lord God said to me", "This is what the Lord Almighty says", "The word of God came unto me". They received revelations from God in visions and dreams (Ezekiel: chapters 40 - 48; Daniel's dream: chapter 7; his visions: chapters 8 – 10; Amos's visions: chapters 8 - 9; Zechariah's visions: chapters 1 - 6.)

Here is what the Fathers say about these different ways of receiving revelations from God.

"If someone suggests that the visions, images and revelations were the work of fantasy and took place in a natural way, he should know that he is far from the truth and the right facts.

For the prophets and also holy hermits living now, who are initiated into the sacred mystery, could see God's revelations not according to the laws of nature, but these were displayed and presented to them supernaturally by the indescribable power and grace of the Holy Spirit, as Basil the Great says, "The prophets could receive revelations in their mind which was pure and not distracted, by an unspeakable power, and they heard the word of God as if proclaimed inside them." Moreover, the prophets could see visions by the action of the Holy Spirit, impressing the images inside their mighty minds. And Gregory the Theologian says, "The Holy Spirit acted first in angels and heavenly creatures, then in fathers and prophets, among whom some could see and know their God, others could predict the future as with the images sent into their mighty minds by the Spirit they could see as if it were in the present." (monks Callistus and Ignatius)

In this excerpt from their writings Callistus and Ignatius do not refer to the prophets' perception of God's revelations through their heart, but through their mind. However we will make it clear later that the Scriptures ascribe to the human heart those very functions which are considered as being of the mind in psychology. It is exactly the heart that is called in the Scripture the organ of the cognition of the Highest.

The Scriptures speak not only of the heart's ability of perceiving the impact of the Spirit of God, but consider the heart to be the core of our spiritual life and Theology, which God Himself improves and corrects.

Here are some fragments which clearly show it.

"And I will give them one heart. And I will distribute a new spirit to their interior. And I will take away the heart of stone from their body. And I will give them a heart of flesh." (Ezek. 11:19)

"And for this reason, you have imparted your fear into our hearts, and also, so that we may call upon your name and may praise you in our captivity, for we are converted from the iniquity of our fathers, who sinned before you." (Baruch 3:7)

"For they reveal the work of the law written in their hearts..." (Rom. 2:15)

"Cast all your transgressions, by which you have transgressed, away from you, and make for yourselves a new heart and a new spirit." (Ezek. 18:31)

"so that the God of our Lord Jesus Christ, the Father of glory, may give a spirit of wisdom and of revelation to you, in knowledge of him.

May the eyes of your heart be illuminated, so that you may know what is the hope of his calling, and the wealth of the glory of his inheritance with the saints," (Eph. 1:17-18)

"Blind the heart of this people. Make their ears heavy and close their eyes, lest they see with their eyes, and hear with their ears, and understand with their heart, and be converted, and then I would heal them." (Is. 6:10)

"...God has sent the Spirit of his Son into your hearts, crying out: "Abba, Father." (Gal. 4:6)

"so that Christ may live in your hearts through a faith..." (Eph. 3:17)

"And so shall the peace of God, which exceeds all understanding, guard your hearts and minds... " (Phil.4:7)

"And I will put my fear into their heart, so that they do not withdraw from me." (Jer. 32:40)

"I will instill my laws in their hearts, and I will inscribe my laws on their minds." (Heb. 10:16)

"...the love of God is poured forth in our hearts through the Holy Spirit..." (Rom. 5:5)

"For God, who told the light to shine out of darkness, has shined a light into our hearts..." (2 Cor. 4:6)

In the Parable of the Sower the Lord himself says that the seed of the Word of God is sown in the man's heart and it is kept by the heart, if the heart is pure, or the seed is snatched by the devil, if the heart can't or is not worthy to keep it.

The highest functions of the human spirit, such as the human faith in God and love for Him, are carried out by the heart.

"For with the heart, we believe unto justice; but with the mouth, confession is unto salvation." (Rom. 10:10)

"...if you believe in your heart..." (Rom. 10:9)

"'You shall love the Lord your God from all your heart..." (Matt. 22:37)

"... For the Lord your God is testing you, so that it may become clear whether or not you love him with all your heart and with all your soul." (Deut. 13:3)

"You shall love the Lord your God with all your heart, and with all your soul, and with all your strength." (Deut. 6:5)

"But sanctify Christ the Lord in your hearts..." (1Pet. 3:15)

We pray with our heart, and one of the greatest kinds of prayer is a soundless cry to God. So Anne, the mother of Samuel the Prophet, prayed to be granted her this great son.

At Mount Sinai, God told Moses: "Why cry out to me?" (Ex. 14:15) And he prayed without words, without moving his lips.

"Their heart cried out to the Lord ...", Jeremiah the Prophet says (Lam. 2:18)

It is well expressed by Landry in his book "The Prayer": "One day an angel said to one of the ardently praying souls: "What are you doing actually? You are shaking the palace of heaven, and nothing can be heard there except your screams." However, the soul did not say a word, only her heart fluttered, and this invisible movement was enough to shake the heights of heaven. "

The Lord Jesus Christ said to us that the heart is a repository of both good and evil: "Progeny of vipers, how are you able to speak good things while you are evil? For out of the abundance of the heart, the mouth speaks.

A good man offers good things from a good storehouse. And an evil man offers evil things from an evil storehouse." (Matt. 12:34-35)

"But what proceeds from the mouth, goes forth from the heart, and those are the things that defile a man.

{15:19} For from the heart go out evil thoughts, murders, adulteries, fornications, thefts, false testimonies, blasphemies." (Matt. 15:18-19)

Our heart is the seat of our conscience, which is like our guardian angel: "For even if our heart reproaches us, God is greater than our heart, and he knows all things." (1 John 3:20)

Speaking about an awesome ability of the heart, Elisha the Prophet said to his servant Gehazi: "Was my heart not present, when the man turned back from his chariot to meet you?" (II Kings 5: 26). So the hearts of deeply loving mothers always follow their children in all their ways though with less prophetic clairvoyance than Elisha's heart had been following Gehazi.

The heart is meant not only for feeling and for communion with God. The Scriptures indicate that it is the body of desire, the source of the will, of good and bad intentions.

"And so, do not choose to judge before the time, until the Lord returns. He will illuminate the hidden things of the darkness, and he will make manifest the decisions of hearts." (1Cor. 4:5)

"My heart has uttered a good word." (Psalm 44(45):1)

"...the will of my heart, and my prayer to God, is for them unto salvation." (Rom. 10:1)

"...desiring to seek his God with his whole heart." (2Chron. 31:21)

"And he went astray by wandering in his heart." (Is. 57:17)

"This most wicked people...walk in the depravity of their own heart..." (Jer. 13:10)

"...until it completes the plan of his heart." (Jer. 23:20)

"...he will grant to you the petitions of your heart." (Ps. (36(37):4)

"...a heart that devises the most wicked thoughts..." (Prov. 6:18)

"...the heart of this people has become incredulous and provocative..." (Jer. 5:23)

"You have granted him the desire of his heart..." (Ps. 20(21):3)

"These have always strayed in heart." (Ps.94(95):10)

"speak peacefully to their neighbor, yet evils are in their hearts." (Ps.27(28):3)

"There are many intentions in the heart of a man." (Prov.19:21) These texts make it evident with perfect clarity that human behaviour, the choice of a way of life is totally determined by desires and aspirations of the heart. We will see later on that the way of thinking is determined by feelings and desires too. But the heart not only determines our thinking; although it may seem strange to all who consider indisputable the teachings of psychology of the mind as an organ of thought and cognition. It is exactly the heart that perceives, thinks and cognizes according to the Scriptures. Let readers not close this book hastily after having read the statement above, which is indeed unacceptable for many. The philosopher Bergson, who in fairness should be considered as one of the greatest thinkers, proclaims the heart to have a prominent role in the process of cognition. Let us however refer to the Scriptures once more:

"But the Lord has not given you an understanding heart..." (Deut. 29:4)

"...every thought of their heart was intent upon evil at all times..." (Gen. 6:5)

"He has scattered the arrogant in the intentions of their heart." (Luke 1:51)

"...perceiving the thoughts of their hearts..." (Luk.9:47)

"...the meditation of my heart will speak prudence." (Ps.48(49):4)

"For the Word of God...discerns the thoughts and intentions of the heart." (Heb. 4:12)

"The things that you say in your hearts..." (Psalm 4:4)

"Why do you think such evil in your hearts?" (Matt. 9:4)

"What are you thinking in your hearts?" (Luke 5:22)

"...some of the scribes were sitting in that place and thinking in their hearts..." (Mark 2:6)

"Now all were thinking about John in their hearts..." (Luke 3:15)

"And I have placed wisdom in the heart of every artisan..." (Ex. 31:6)

" If wisdom is to enter into your heart..." (Prov. 2:10)

" In the heart of the prudent, wisdom finds rest." (Prov. 14:33)

"...when the hearts of the sons of men are filled with malice and contempt in their lives..." (Eccles. 9:3)

"And the heart of the foolish will understand knowledge..." (Is. 32:4)

"...the thoughts of many hearts may be revealed." (Luke 2:35)

"...why do these thoughts rise up in your hearts?" (Luke 24:38)

Let us ponder the last sentence. How do these thoughts enter your hearts? Where do they come from? If the thought "enters", it means that it is not born in the heart.

Certainly, the Scriptures do not contradict indisputable physiological facts and do not deny the role of the brain in thinking; not only in thinking but in all psychical processes. In the above mentioned words of the monks Callistus and Ignatius, St. Basil the Great and Gregory the Theologian, the prophecies and the visions are seen as being caused by the graceful impact of the Holy Spirit on the mind of the prophets, and the mental processes take place in the brain. However the process of thinking is not limited by the activity of the cerebral cortex only and takes place also elsewhere. We know which parts of the brain are responsible for the motoric, sensory, vasomotoric, respiratory, thermal and other functions, but there is no area in the brain which is responsible for the feelings. Nobody could find in the brain the centres of joy and sorrow, anger and fear, the aesthetic and religious feelings.

Although all the sensors and all organs of the body in general are connected to the brain cells by means of the nerve fibres, these are the visual and auditory, olfactory and gustatory, tactile and thermal, locomotory, and many others kinds of sensations only. They are however, just sensations. Not making a distinction between sensations and feelings results in the greatest psychological mistake.

If we could, by way of speaking, stop the most high-speed and complex dynamics of mental processes and analyse the individual elements in their static state, then sensations would appear to us only as initial impulses for the emergence of thoughts, feelings, desires and volitional movements. And a single thought isolated from the brain would be just an unfinished raw material destined for the deep final tempering inside the heart, which is the crucible of emotions and will.

We do not know how exactly the thoughts arising in the brain are transmitted to the heart, but the thought being a purely psychological action as opposed to sensation, which is a physiological action, does not need the anatomic paths of transmission. The feelings arising in the heart, depending on one or other thought, and forming these thoughts to a major extent do not need these paths either.

The heart receives these processed thoughts and sensory perceptions not only from the brain but itself has a wonderful and most important ability to receive exogenous feelings of the highest order from the spiritual world, not at all appropriate to the organs of the senses.

And these feelings from the heart are transmitted to the mind, the brain and to a large extent determine, direct, and modify all mental processes, which take place in the human mind and spirit.

Let us review some of the previous quotations:

"...the thoughts of many hearts may be revealed." (Luke 2:35)
" In the heart of the prudent, wisdom finds rest." (Prov. 14:33)
"...when the hearts of the sons of men are filled with malice and contempt in their lives..." (Eccles. 9:3)

If it is possible to speak of "the thoughts of the heart" and of the heart as the accumulator and dwelling of wisdom, it means that not only the thoughts born in the mind become sensually and volitionally completed in the heart; and not only the exogenous spiritual impacts are perceived by the heart and transmitted to the brain. In addition to it those exogenous impacts give rise to thoughts and reflections in the heart, just as the impulses of the organs of the senses are the stimulants and at the same time the material for the mental activity of the brain. Therefore the heart is the second organ of perception, cognition and thought, wisdom abides in it. However if the heart is deprived of the grace of God and does not perceive the promptings of the Spirit of truth and goodness from the transcendent world, and is inclined to perception of the spirit of evil, lies and pride, then insanity arises in the heart and lives in it.

Intellectuals take for an indisputable truth the statement that we cognize reality through the mind, of which the anatomical and physiological body is, naturally, they say, the brain.

But already in the XVIIth century, at the height of Cartesian dogmatism, when intellectualism was all-powerful, a brilliant mathematician and philosopher Blaise Pascal was able to discover the limit and the impotence of the mind, and proposed to replace it with cognitive ability, which would distinguish itself by directness and the ability of studying the truth.

An ability to which Bergson later gave a definite name "intuition", Pascal called a sense of subtleties, flair of judgment, a feeling, an inspiration, the heart, an instinct. In his "Thoughts" all these terms signify identically the direct cognition of reality, awareness of a living reality, which is opposite to the knowledge through reason and rational calculations. Pascal in his very first works set the new difference between a "geometrical mind" and flair for subtleties.

A "geometrical mind" is exactly what we call the rationalistic or logical way of thinking, while intuitive thinking is a sense of subtleties.

"Reason", Pascal writes, "acts slowly, taking into account so many of the principles that should always be [actively] present that it is constantly tired and distracted, unable to hold them together. Sense works differently: it operates instantaneously and it is always ready to act. So we should lay our hope in feelings; otherwise our hope will always be unsteady."

Then his famous statement follows: "The heart has its reasons of which reason knows nothing". And then Pascal says in addition, "It is the heart which perceives God and not the reason."

The idea of cognition and of the great variety of our spiritual life, which is given to us in the Scriptures, is not compatible at all with intellectualism, that is the philosophical doctrine asserting that every reality can be cognized, and this can be accomplished through the cognitive ability of the mind only.

Intellectualism considers free, speculative cognition as a human activity, which belongs to the domain of perfection, and even as the only activity, worthy of man. But what is even more the core of intellectualism is that it recognizes the reality of things only in so far as it can be accepted by reason.

What on earth can be compared to the pretentiousness of this proud doctrine which denies the reality of everything that does not fit in our poor and very limited reason? The intellectualists ignore all that is so clearly and undoubtedly perceived by our heart from the transcendental world, everything that is cognized through Pascal's "sense of subtleties".

It was however the ancient philosopher Epicurus who said that all the objects of perception are true and real, which is the same as saying that something is true and that it exists.

Why would the perceptions of the Highest through the heart be not true then?

It is only the brain which is considered as the organ of reason and will, while the spinal cord is said to be a system of pathways and an organ for instinctive and trophic activity.

However, a beheaded frog, when its skin is irritated, will act in a way to avoid irritation. If the irritation continues, it tries to run away and to hide in the same way as a frog with a head.

In the wars of ants which have no brain, a premeditation is clearly revealed, and therefore a reason, which is no different to the human one.

It is perfectly obvious that not only the brain but also the ganglion of insects as well as the spinal cord and the sympathetic nervous system of vertebrates are the body of the will.

It is impossible to expound even the basic idea of the amazing and deep philosophy of life of Henri Bergson in a small theological treatise.

I can only say that he has shown a completely new way of understanding life. At the same time he exposed the complete inability of the philosophy of rationalism (intellectualism?) with regard to this.

Not only Pascal was a great forerunner of Bergson on this revolutionary path of philosophy. Similar to Bergson's method of cognition is Maine de Biran's method of introspection for the investigation of reality in the human consciousness. He thinks that it is impossible to "grasp" reality in any other way than in "one's living self". Neither keen observations [of the outside world-Translator], nor rational thinking can give us this.

Schopenhauer was the first to prove that a concept, invented by reason, working idly as in a vacuum, can't be anything else but meaningless chimeras, fit only to meet the demands of the "professors of philosophy"; that the mind has forms only, and is "a meaningless ability." He considers intuition to be a counterbalance to reason.

Bergson expressed amazing and quite new statements about the idol of the intellectualists, the brain. He believes that the difference between the spinal cord, which reacts reflexively to the impulses, and the brain, is not in the nature of their functions, but in the degree of their complexity only.

The brain just registers the perception coming from outside and selects the appropriate method of response. Bergson says, "The brain is nothing but a sort of telephone exchange: its role is merely to issue a message or to clarify it." It adds nothing to what is receives.

All the organs of the senses are connected to the brain by nerve fibres, it shelters the motorial system, and it is a centre, where the external stimulation comes in contact with one or another mechanism of motorial reflection.

The brain shows by its very structure that its function is the responding in an appropriate way to a stimulus from outside. Afferent nerve fibres, which conduct the impulses from the organs of sense, end in cells of the sensory zone in the cerebral cortex. These cells are, in their turn, connected through the other fibres to the cells of the motorial zones, thus transmitting the impulses to them. As the number of these interconnections is countless, the brain has an endless ability to modify its reaction to an external stimulation, and acts as a kind of switchboard.

The nervous system and particularly the brain are not devices of ideal thinking and cognition, but only the tools that are meant for use in action.

"The brain is not an organ of thought, feeling, consciousness, but it is what chains the mind, feelings and thoughts to real life, forcing them to listen to the real needs and make them capable of expedient action."

The brain, in fact, is the organ of attention to life, of adaptation to a reality. (The Body and the Soul. You and the Life. 1921 December 20)

This is amazing enough, but these overwhelming thoughts of the great metaphysician almost completely coincide with the new doctrine of higher nervous activity, created by our brilliant physiologist Ivan Petrovich Pavlov.

More so, we can say that Henri Bergson just before Pavlov, had by pure philosophical thinking, realized the essence of Pavlov's physiological teachings based on experimental study of conditioned reflexes of the brain.

To substantiate this position, I shall give a few excerpts from Pavlov's book "Twenty years of experience of objective study of higher nervous activity in animals", but first I need to explain what are what Pavlov calls "conditioned reflexes", and "analyzers". Each animal has a permanent set of congenital reflexes that Pavlov calls "unconditional". For example, an animal immediately rushes to the food it sees, it pulls back its leg if the leg is irritated; a snail retracts into its shell when touched; a newborn baby makes sucking movements when touching the mother's breast with his lips.

But besides these unconditioned reflexes, higher animals, namely dogs, with which Pavlov experimented, can also gain new, artificially developed reflexes, which Pavlov calls "conditional", and which can be called also temporary or acquired. For example, if in a series of experiments a dog is irritated with something a short time before receiving food, such as a sharp sound , a light signal, scratching its skin, then soon this arbitrary, "conditioned" stimulus will effect the animal in the same way as the sight and the smell of meat (an "unconditioned" stimulus): the dog immediately starts salivating and has a motorial reaction, appropriate to a dog when seeing food. The "conditioned" signal led to the formation of a new, temporary, "conditional" reflex.

How exactly are these [conditional] reflexes formed?

When the cells of the eye, sensitive to light, are touched by light, the sensitive cells of the organ of hearing by sound, the sensitive ends of the nerves of the skin by touch, the corresponding sensations are transmitted by the nerve fibres into the areas of the cerebral cortex, the nerve cells of which are meant specifically for the perception of these stimuli (e.g. the optic nerve is located in the occipitalis parts of the hemispheres, the sound nerve in the temporal part, etc.)

The nerve cells of the cortex, upon receiving a stimulus, analyse it, and according to the results, transfer impulses to the lower centres of the brain and spinal cord for a corresponding executive action (effect): the motorial or vasomotorial one, secretion etc.

These downstream executive centres are called effectors.

Pavlov gave the name "analyst" to the entire system consisting of specific, perceiving cells of a sensory organ, the fibres of sensory nerves connected to them, and their extensions, the fibres of the white matter, which end in the nerve cells of the sensory parts in the cortex. There is a countless multitude of such analysts in the cortex.

Among them, besides these analysts, which have their beginning in the cells of each of our five senses, there are plenty of other analysts, which are connected to all the organs of our body and thus transmit to the brain cortex in the hemispheres information about what goes on inside the body.

Thus, the brain is responsible for the huge task of analysing all these stimuli and responding to them by the reactions of the effectors.

The following excerpts from Pavlov's book are now clear:

"In terms of conditioned reflexes, the cerebral hemispheres are a set of analysts which have the task of decomposing the complexity of the inner and outer world into separate elements and moments and then relate this multitude to the diverse activities of the organism."

"The large hemisphere is an organ of the animal organism, which specializes in continuous implementation of an ever more perfect balance of the organism with the environment; it is the organ of an adequate and immediate response to different combinations and variations of the phenomena of the external world; it is to some extent a special organ for the continuous development of an animal organism".

"The motorial part of the cerebral hemispheres is a receptor area, or the main area, and motorial effects during stimulation of the cortex are reflective by nature. The cerebral cortex, thus, is only a receptor apparatus, which analyses and synthetizes the incoming stimuli in a variety of manners. The stimuli reach the effectors through the downward leading connective fibres."

There are no mechanisms in the front lobes that are supreme with regard to the totality of the hemispheres. There can be no question of any general mechanisms which are settled in the front lobes. There are no particularly important devices there which would be responsible for the highest perfection of nervous activity". Pavlov, like Bergson, suggests that the difference between the brain and the spinal cord is in their complexity only, not in the nature of their functions. He and his school believe it is possible to attribute the deciphered patterns of the higher nervous activity of dogs, which was obtained during the experiments with conditioned reflexes, to the physiology of the human brain.

A dog can only get secondary conditioned reflexes based on the primary ones, whereas a monkey has a number of secondary reflexes more; for humans, without doubt, a very large amount of acquired reflexes, overlapping the previous ones, is possible. This ongoing formation of new, ever more complex interconnections inside the brain in the course of a human life, gives the opportunity of improving the mental performance and expanding consciousness. Nevertheless this complicated brain activity remains in essence just reflexes of the brain. This new view on the physiology of the brain, we think, should replace the current doctrine of associations in psychology.

But it is as Bergson said: "The brain is nothing but a sort of central telephone exchange: its role is just to deliver a message or to clarify it. It adds nothing to what is received," isn't it?

The research by Pavlov and his staff on the physiological significance of the frontal lobes of the brain hemispheres has an overwhelming importance. These were hitherto regarded by all as the most important part of the brain, the centres of higher mental activity, the organ of thought "par excellence", even "the seat of the soul." But Pavlov did not find there "any particularly important devices which could provide the highest perfection of the nervous activity," and the cortex in the front parts of the cerebral hemispheres, as well as the rest of the cortex, is just a sensor area. The entire cortex, the most perfect part of the brain, consists of an innumerable multitude of analysts, analysts and more analysts. And if there is no room for any kind of centre of feelings in the cortex, it is even more improbable that it can be situated in the gray nodes of the brain stem, which, as we partly know, have purely physiological functions. The cerebral cortex analyses not feelings, but sensations.

And the fact that the brain can't be considered an organ of feelings, confirms to a large extent the teaching of the Scriptures on the heart as the organ of feelings in general, and especially the higher feelings.

These conclusions of Pavlov's studies match the observations of surgeons on many wounded with abscesses on the frontal lobes. They usually are not accompanied by any noticeable mental disorder or changes in the higher cognitive functions. I will just give two clear observations from my own experience.

I removed about 50 cubic centimetres of purulence from a huge abscess, which undoubtedly destroyed the entire left frontal lobe of a young wounded man, and I noticed absolutely no psychiatric defects after this operation.

I can say the same about the other patient operated on for large cysts of the meninges. When opening wide his skull I was surprised to see that almost the entire right half of it was empty, and that all the right hemisphere of the brain was squeezed and almost impossible to discern.

So, if the brain can't be regarded as an organ of feelings and the exclusive authority of higher cognition, it confirms to a large extent the teaching of the Scriptures about the heart as an organ of feelings in general, and especially of the highest feelings.

Chapter 3. The Brain and the Spirit. The Spirit in Nature

"We are still convinced that the mind is an attribute of the brain, and subordination of the mind to the brain seems to us so obvious that we can't think of one without the other. And hence, by authority of a mistaken synthesis, we conclude that body and spirit are mutually subordinate to one another. This is because we are used to confuse the mind and the spirit. The mind, of course, is not the spirit, but only a manifestation of the spirit. The mind refers to the spirit as a part to the whole. The spirit is much more extensive than the mind, but due to the invariable intellectualistic concept we see the whole spirit in the mind"(Frank Granhman).

"The spirit projects outside the brain from all sides. Activity of the brain is limited to the transformation of a small portion of what is happening in the mind, into motion" (Bergson, "Creative Evolution").

What do we know about the spirit? We know much from the Scriptures, and not a little about the phenomena of the spirit in nature and man.

1. St. Sergius of Radonezh was having a meal with the brethren of his monastery. Suddenly he stood up, bowed to the west and said, "And you too rejoice, pastor of Christ's flock, and the blessing of the Lord be with you." The brethren asked in amazement: "Who are you speaking to, Holy Father?" St. Sergius answered, "About eight miles away from our monastery Bishop Stephan of Perm, stopped on his way to Moscow. He bowed to the Holy Trinity and said," "Peace to you, brother in spirit." So I answered him." Some of the monks rushed to the place and caught up with St. Stephen. He confirmed what was said by St. Sergius.

2. An engineer and staunch materialist, K.I. Pearl, parted from his friend K., who left for Moscow, while he lived in Tashkent with another engineer. One day at three o"clock in the night he was awakened by a loud shout: "Karl Ivanovich!" He lit a candle and woke his lover. They both searched the whole apartment, but found nobody. In extreme astonishment he noted the date of this strange event. A week later he received a message about the suicide of his ex-friend K. that had taken place that very night and hour he had heard the mysterious call. The death call of the suicide, full of anguish and love instantly covered a distance of 3300 km and was perceived by the brain of the sleeping K.I. Pearl.

3. Mrs Green, sitting in the verandah of her house after dinner in a town in England, suddenly had a vision: a cabriolet with two young women in it was approaching the steep bank of a lake; one of the wheels of the cabriolet suddenly broke, and the cabriolet with horses and passengers fell into the lake; they were drowning, and at the same moment Mrs. Green heard her name, cried out in an appeal full of despair. A month later she received a letter from her brother, describing the death of his daughter and her friend just as she had seen it in her vision.

I have borrowed the last example from a very interesting book of academician Charles Richet, a famous physiologist and physicist, one of the most prominent figures in the field of metapsychology, a new science that emerged at the end of the last century. It is now being developed by renowned scientists in different countries. The aim of metapsychology is the investigation by all the scientific methods available of the unexplained and mysterious psychic phenomena labelled by the official psychology as superstitions and fairy tales.

But it can only be rejected by those who are biased or not familiar with it or haven't studied it with the deep scientific objectivity of C. Richet, Oliver Lodge and other eminent scientists, who have created a wide literature on metapsychology. There are very many similar facts to be found in Richet's book, each more surprising than the other. He analyses the facts with great scientific rigour, and he comes to the following conclusion: "There are vibrations (forces) in the universe, which excite our sensitivity and thus give us a trustworthy knowledge of reality, which our normal senses can't give. These forces, new and strange, will create a revolution in psychology and rebuild it from the ground."

Dr. Kotik, who has written a significant book on his experience with thought transmission ("The Emanation of Psychic-Physic Energy", Wiesbaden, 1908), explains them as follows: "A thought is an energy radiated outwards. It has physical and psychic properties, and it can be called psychic-physical energy. This energy born in the brain spreads itself through the entire body and the limbs. It can pass through metal conductors but it is difficult to transmit it through the air. Apparently, it is not specifically attributed to the thought; it may be, that all things emit some kind of vibrant energy, for sensitive subjects not only perceive what the experimenter thinks, but they also recognize material objects, which do not think."

What gives Dr. Kotik reason to believe that the invisible radiation of energy in a thinking brain is not only mental, but also psychic-physical? It is just the fact that when you connect the experimentist to the sensitive subject with a metal wire, the sensor reads thoughts a little better.

But a huge number of other facts described by Richet show that even without any contact the transmission of an unknown energy takes place. It is only due to our ineradicable habit to explain the incomprehensible and the unknown with the understandable (intellectually) and the known that this energy is thought to be material vibrations, which are caused by the molecular fluctuations of the brain substance, which fluctuations are also still unknown.

Those who accept the primitive explanation are quite satisfied when they are told that their brain emanates some electric vibrations.

Why, however, should we not recognize, along with Richet, that inexplicable, even bizarre, as he says, forces, quite unknown to us in the present state of science, are the basis of the phenomena of telepathy (the transfer of thoughts and feelings at a distance) and clairvoyance? Anyone who reads his big book gets the shock of his life.

I believe that for the present we have the right to come to just one but very important conclusion: in addition to normal stimuli, which are adequate to our sensor organs, our brain and heart can receive much more important stimuli coming from the brain and heart of other people, animals, and all of nature around us and, what is the most important, from the transcendental world unknown to us.

By what, if not by forces of transcendental order, can such facts as reported by Richet, be explained?

1. M. Hialon confirmed the trustworthiness of a strange story which had happened to M.M. Greedy, the director of the Daily Telegraph. When one Sunday he was standing in St. John's Church, he suddenly felt a very powerful suggestion. It was something like a voice saying to him: "Return to your editorial office." The order was so overbearing that M.M. Greedy ran through the whole church like a madman, through the streets, rushed into the editorial office to the amazement of his employees, and flung open its door. The kerosene lamp on his desk was shooting large flames and the whole room was filled with smoke.

2. Mrs Tomeli in San Martin, one night trying to fall asleep, suddenly saw her son being run over by a carriage and dying.

She ran during the storm 5 miles down the road in Costa de Borge and found her son in the ditch next next to the road.

3. The famous William James quotes the following case: Bertha, a young girl, disappeared on the 31st of October 1898 in Enfield. More than 100 people were sent to search the woods and the lake shore. It was known that she went to the bridge, and since then nobody had seen her. The diver who had searched for her in the lake could not find her. But in the night of 3rd of January, a woman who lived 8 km away from Enfield saw in her dream Bertha's body in a certain place. In the morning she went to the bridge and showed the diver the exact spot where he would find Bertha's body. According to her instructions the diver found her lying upside down and well hidden. The body was at a depth of 6 meters in the snags, and at first he could see only a rubber shoe on her foot. "I was shocked", the diver said, "I'm not afraid of dead bodies in the water, but I was afraid of the woman standing on the bridge. How is it possible that she came here from somewhere 8 km away to show where the body was? It was lying in a deep hole, upside down. The water was so dark that I could see nothing. "

The last two examples belong to the area of clairvoyance, to which Richet gave a new name - kriptosteziya. This term describes well the following extraordinary facts.

1. In Blueau prison a prisoner hanged himself with his tie. Dr. Dufali cut a piece of this tie, wrapped it in several layers of paper and gave it to a clairvoyant (not a professional one) called Mary. She said there was something wrapped in a paper that killed a man, a rope... not a rope but a tie; a prisoner who had killed a man hanged himself with it. She said the man was killed with an axe, and pointed out the place where the axe was thrown. Indeed, the axe was found in this place.

2. Charles Richet met his friend Stella, a young girl on the 2nd of December and said to her, "I'm going to give a lecture on

snake venom." Stella, showing an astonishing clairvoyance several times before, replied immediately: "Last night I saw serpents, or rather, eels." Without of course mentioning the reason I asked her to tell me the dream. And these were exactly her words: "It was more likely two eels than serpents, because I saw they had a bright white belly and a sticky skin. And I said to myself, I really do not like these animals, but I hate them being tortured."

This dream coincided amazingly with what I had done the day before, on the 1st of December. On that day, I was experimenting with eels. To take their blood, I put two eels on the table. I remembered their glossy white belly and sticky skin. They were attached to the table to take out their heart. I had not seen Stella for a long time and certainly had not talked to her about it, and she had had no contact with people who visit my laboratory.

Discussing many facts similar to the above mentioned Richet concludes that all people, even the apparently least sensitive, have other capacities of cognition in addition to the common ones. But these capacities are extremely weak, almost imperceptible, to non-sensitive people. The thoughts of a person may in a mysterious way appear in the minds of others. We are not isolated but we are, in an unfathomable way all connected together. And certainly there is some truth in what is called "mass-hysteria". A powerful stream of sympathy or anger, indignation or enthusiasm leads to an almost complete unity of people gathered in a theatre, a market or a parliament. It is a kind of stream which sweeps everything away. Why couldn't we consider the unifying work of emotion in a crowd and the transmission of ideas in Richet's experiments as the same phenomenon? The selfless act of one brave man can inspire a whole army. This powerful flow of the spirit of bravery and courage, emanatingfrom one ardent heart, kindles the hearts of hundreds of others who receive it as an antenna receives radio waves. What, if not a powerful spiritual energy, should we call this all-prevailing power, which generated global psychic epidemics in the Middle Ages and recklessly and irrepressibly gathered hundreds of thousands of people in the crusades?!

Isn't it clear that a flow of an evil power, an evil spirit is poured into our hearts and brains when we see the face of our enemy, distorted by hatred, his eyes casting sparks and making our heart shrink in fear?

The love of a mother flows quietly and sweetly into her child that is clinging to her chest; the passionate feelings of a loving husband flows powerfully onto his wife. Quiet and joyful light illuminates the soul of the man who does the works of love and mercy, when the grace of God touches it.

What is this but the spiritual energy of love?

"I will pour out my spirit upon all flesh..." (Joel 2:28) God is spirit. God is love, and the outpouring of His Spirit is the outpouring of His love onto all the living. Love creates. The all-creating and all-consuming, endless stream of spiritual energy of God's love created the Universe. It was created out of nothing, in that sense that there was no such thing as the primary... (may be "matter", an omission in the original text. ed.). There is no eternal matter, the same as there is no matter at all, and there is only energy in its various forms, and when condensed it is matter.

Matter represents a stable form of inter-atomic energy, and heat, light, electricity are the unstable forms of the same energy. The core of the process of disintegration of atoms, i.e. the break-up of the matter, is a modification in the state of the inter-atomic energy from stable equilibrium to an unstable one, which we perceive as electricity, light, heat, etc. The matter is thus gradually transformed into energy.

In the first chapter we have said that by the atomic break-up the still more subtle forms of energy, close to something immaterial are liberated.

What hampers us taking the final step and recognizing the existence of a fully immaterial, spiritual energy, and considering it as the primary form, the mother and the source of all forms of physical energy? Only an a priori rejection of the Spirit and the spiritual world, a stubborn and incomprehensible denial, in spite of all the facts that imperatively compel us to reckon with them and recognize a limitless, far more important spiritual world along with the material one.

"O how good and gracious, Lord, is your spirit in all things!" (Wis. Sol. 12:1)

"Do I not fill up heaven and earth, says the Lord?" (Jer. 23:24)

"But, if he directs his heart towards him, he will draw his spirit and breath to himself.

All flesh will fail together, and man will return to ashes." (Job 34:14-15)

"But if you turn your face away, they will be disturbed. You will take away their breath, and they will fail, and they will return to their dust.

You will send forth your Spirit, and they will be created. And you will renew the face of the earth." (Ps.103(104):29-30)

"It is the Spirit who gives life." (John 6:64)

"In his hand is the soul of all the living and the spirit of all the flesh of mankind." (Job 12:10)

"Yet the stars have given light from their posts, and they rejoiced.

They were called, and so they said, "Here we are," and they shined with cheerfulness to him who made them." (Baruch 3:34)

"The beauty of the desert will fatten, and the hills will be wrapped with exultation.
The rams of the sheep have been clothed, and the valleys will abound with grain. They will cry out; yes, they will even utter a hymn." (Ps.64(65):13,14)
And many of the Psalms and the Song of Hananiah, Mishael and Azariah, are full of the spirit of hylozoism.
The idea of the universal realization and quickening by the Spirit of God is shown quite clearly in all these texts from the Scriptures. It is impossible to speak of a "dead nature." There are no distinct boundaries between inorganic and organic nature. This is also the point of view of modern science.
A vivid evidence of this is given by the philosophy of Fichte and Lotze, and the great profundity of Leibniz. These are Leibniz's words, coinciding with the texts of Holy Scripture:
"There would be a gap in the creation, if the nature of matter were the opposite to that of the spirit. Those who deny the existence of a soul in animals, and imagination and life in general in the other bodies do not acknowledge the Divine power, because they invent something incongruous with God and with nature, an absolute lack of forces, a kind of metaphysical void, which is as absurd as the empty space or a physical emptiness. "
Countless stars and planets rush in eternity through the space, never slowing down their movement. It is only through the power of this movement that incredibly heavy bodies are kept in space, like a heavy 40-inch shell can keep rushing along its trajectory through the air.
Myriads of stars, planets, asteroids, meteors and comets rush through space. The face of the earth is changed by blowing winds, water flowing, the friction of sliding glaciers, temperature fluctuations, the waves' surf. The powerful movement of underground volcanic forces creates new ranges of mountains and precipices on earth.

During the centuries of movement innumerable worlds and stars are destroyed and created again; there exists a great process of evolution, the highest order movement in the universe. Atoms and electrons are moving infinitely almost with the speed of light, like X-rays, ions, and all the products of the dissociation of matter, which always takes place. Life of the organisms is sustained by the continuous motion of molecules in the organism's cells. The thought of a man is followed by molecular motion in the nerve cells. There is no motionlessness even in death, which is nothing but a certain change in the instantaneous states of equilibrium, which are of a short duration also.

If it is so obvious that motion is the essence and the fundamental law of material nature, it is hardly possible that this universal law would not reign also in the spiritual life.

The principal law of the entire nature, the whole law of motion wipes away the boundary between the living and the dead. Motion is the essence of matter. And if we want to assume that motion in the living organisms, which is the basis of their psychic phenomena, is generated and determined by the energy of the spirit of life, we must admit then that the motion of inorganic nature is a derivative of the same spirit. Spiritual energy emanated by the Spirit of God, the energy of love drives forward the entire nature and "quickens" all and everything.

It is the source of life, and nothing is dead.

Motion in the inorganic nature is a manifestation of life, though at the lowest level, about which we know little. The existing genetic link between inorganic and organic nature proves it. For the life of plants starts in the soil, and serves as food for the entire animal kingdom. Both inorganic and organic nature are created from the same chemical elements and according to the same physical laws.

One great universal law of development governs the whole of Universe, and the development can not be stopped, and there can not be a sharp boundary between the "dead" nature and the world of living beings. And the most striking feature of living nature, its being animated is not something which appears suddenly at its boundary with inorganic nature. Spiritual energy permeates all inorganic nature, the entire Universe. But this energy reaches the level of a free, self-conscious spirit in the higher forms of development (creation) only.

Sensitivity is inherent in all living things. However, the exact methods of research show that matter is not only extremely mobile (mercury in the thermometer rises at the touch of a hand), but that it has an unconscious sensitivity, superior to the conscious one of living beings.

The bolometer, comprising a platinum plate as its substantial part, is so sensitive that it reacts to the impact of a very weak beam of light, which raises the temperature only one hundred millionth fraction of a degree. Stele showed that touching an iron wire with a finger is enough for an electrical current to appear. It is known that the Hertz waves deeply influence metals at a distance of hundreds of kilometres, causing electrical fluctuations in them. The wireless telegraphy is based on this phenomenon. In his ingenious experiments Stele showed that metals may become "tired" and that after "relaxing" this "tiredness" disappears, that poisons can "irritate" and "supress" them.

Living things differ from the "dead" nature because of the fact that they feed themselves and multiply. Science didn't discover these properties in the minerals. , but there are indications that these functions are inherent in them. There is nevertheless reason to expect that in the future science will find evidence of it in nature. An enzyme has already been found in certain minerals, which is similar in its effect to sexual hormones, accelerating the growth and sexual maturation of newborn animals. And we know that in living organisms the enzymes mainly serve the purposes of feeding. What is so strange about the assumption that the mineral enzymes are necessary for the feeding of minerals, of course not as in a living organism, but in some way, not yet known to us?

Doesn't the chemical metabolism which always takes place in the inorganic nature have the role of nutrition? Isn't the soil thirsty, isn't it in need of water like all living beings? A mineral substance is characterized by its crystalline form the same as a living creature by its anatomical structure. Before reaching its definite shape, a crystal passes through consistent evolutionary steps like a living creature and a plant: it begins in a granular state, which becomes fibrous, and finally, homogeneous.

Like animals and plants, disfigured crystal corrects its damage. Every crystal is an organized being. Crystals have two forms of reproduction. In certain circumstances, for example at a certain pressure, concentration of the solution, etc., the liquid can crystallize only when the crystal nucleus is added. The resulting crystals then can be considered descendants of the crystal, just as bacteria that develop in the solution are the descendants of the bacteria that we have introduced into this solution. However, there may be such conditions in an environment which allow crystallization to take place without the initiating "embryos".

It is necessary to think about the depth of Joel's words: "I will pour out my spirit upon all flesh." (Joel 2:28)

Precise and deeply important is the relationship between the spirit and the form. The spirit inherent in matter is clearly reflected in the forms generated by this matter. And more than that, the spirit creates the forms.

This is clearly expressed in the forms of the human body, although they do not always correspond to the spiritual nature of a man. Not only the eyes are the mirror of the soul, but all forms of the body and its movements correspond to the soul, the spirit, the same as the image of an evil man described by Solomon (Prov. 6:12-14). A man's entire appearance clearly reflects his spiritual essence. A rough and brutal spirit as early as the embryogenesis directs the development of somatic cells and creates gross and repulsive forms which correspond to it. A pure and gentle spirit creates a dwelling for itself which is full of beauty and tenderness. Think of the Madonnas by Raphael and Leonardo da Vinci's Mona Lisa.

What, if not the shaping influence of the spirit, can explain the amazing subtle differences between two very similar faces, especially between women's faces? They might have the same outlines of nose, mouth, almost an equal size and proportions of face and head, while one face is vulgar, and the other is refined and beautiful.

A careful analysis shows that this difference in the spiritual image of almost identical physical forms depends on very small and delicate variations: a slightly different outline of the eyebrows, of the fold of the lips, an almost indiscernible difference in the size of the eye socket and shape indicates a very different spiritual image. A striking image of Mona Lisa was created by the subtle features that Leonardo da Vinci was adding to this woman's face in the course of several years.

This is exactly how the spiritual energy inherent in the chromosomes of germ cells acts in the embryonic development and creates vivid images of beauty or ugliness; tenderness, purity and love or rudeness, repulsively dominating animal instincts and malice. These innate external forms become still more evident in the postembryonic life corresponding to the development of the spirit in one direction or another. The value of beauty in nature is versatile, and, of course, it is not limited only to the purposes of sexual selection. Male birds sing beautifully and wear bright and beautiful plumage not only to attract females. The shining beauty and fragrance of flowers is not only to attract the insects which bear the fertilizing pollen. The great beauty of nature doesn't only have utilitarian purposes of course.

Compositions and elements of beauty and ugliness in nature are perceived and transformed by the human spirit into works of art and science: the two great engines of the spiritual development of mankind. From the simplest forms of beauty, from a roundness and smoothness of lines pleasant to the eyes, proportion and symmetry of form, beauty and strength of light and shade, a harmonious combination of colours and sounds, nature reaches the heights of the grand picture of beauty, full of spiritual power and greatness.

Dark clouds covering the mountain chains and cliffs, huge ocean waves driven by the wind, storming the coastal cliffs, are full of the spirit of an immense power. The spirit of eternity and infinity is poured into our souls from the myriads of stars in the night sky. The gentle colours of the dawn and the fields and the lakes, illuminated by moonlight evoke joy and peace. Nature shows the supreme value of moral beauty in the meek and pure eyes of good men and the loathsomeness of disgraceful things in the repulsive appearance of villains and dishonest people.

And if it is so obvious that in the forms of moral beauty or disgrace we actually perceive the emanations of the spirit of beauty or the spirit of evil that stir our hearts, then why can't we state that the perception of beauty and ugliness in inorganic nature, is a similar effect of spiritual energy inherent in all nature, on our soul?

It does not matter that shapeless amorphous matter does not produce such an impression of spiritual order on us; it is important that the Spirit is associated with form. We say that the Spirit governs the development of human bodies in the forms respective to their kind. All forms of the Universe, including inorganic nature, are built under the creative influence of the spirit. Therefore the purpose and the meaning of beauty should be seen in the deep spiritual, even moral influence on human souls, produced by the spiritual energy of nature's beauty. If the universe were what it appears to be to the materialists, there would not be the beauty of forms created by the spirit in it.

I was brought a bouquet of flowers. O how much subtle, charming beauty is there in these marvellous little creatures of God! They are also charming in their small, meek simplicity. The finest lace of delicate white blossoms, little pink, purple and blue creatures look at us with the pure eyes of their petals and corolla, and pour their wonderful fragrance over us.

Isn't it obvious that this is a silent sermon on the purity of the soul? One must have a very rough heart in order not to hear this voice of God, so clearly sounding in the beauty of the material forms of nature. It is natural that women are particularly fond of flowers, and this fact speaks in favour of their hearts.

Chapter 4. The Spirit of Plants and Animals

The fact that animals possess a spirit is clearly testified by the Scriptures. Here are the texts to prove it:

"Who knows if the spirit of the sons of Adam ascend upward, and if the spirit of the beasts descend downward?" (Eccles. 3:21).

"O most strong One, the God of the spirits of all flesh..." (Num. 16:22)

"Therefore, the Lord God, having formed from the soil all the animals of the earth and all the flying creatures of the air, brought them to Adam, in order to see what he would call them. For whatever Adam would call any living creature, that would be its name." (Gen. 2:19).

"For the life of the flesh is in the blood, and I have given it to you, so that you may atone with it upon the altar for your souls, and so that the blood may be for an expiation of the soul.

For this reason, I have said to the sons of Israel: No soul among you shall eat blood, nor among the newcomers who sojourn with you." (Lev. 17:11,12)

Blood of an animal sacrificed is holy and sanctifying, because the animal's soul, breath of the Holy Spirit, dwells in it. Therefore it is forbidden to use it in food.

"It is the Spirit who gives life." (John 6:64)

"... the spirit of life from God entered into them." (Rev. 11:11)

In our prayer to the Holy Spirit we call Him the giver of life. And if even in inorganic nature the presence of the Spirit is so evident, then, of course, all plants and animals must be considered spiritualized. Of all the gifts of the Holy Spirit the most common in nature is the spirit of life, and it is, of course, inherent not only in animals but in plants, too. Indians and other peoples of Asia differ from the Europeans in their views on plants. They recognize deeply the spirituality of the plants. Plants with their entire being take in avidly light, air, moisture, which their whole life depends upon. They clearly enjoy light, wind, dew and rain. Why not admit that they brightly perceive and feel these sources of their life and joy, but the way they do it may be quite different from a man or an animal, whose need of light is not so vital. The plant feels probably much deeper than an animal all the finest qualities of the soil, in which rich branches of its roots exist, on which, together with the light and air, depends its whole life. We know how delicately different plants select from the soil nutrients necessary specifically for them and not for the other plants. Isn't it irrefutable that this plant should have a very special kind of sensitivity, which neither animals nor humans have? (Fechner)

"Nerves can't be considered a necessary substratum of spiritual life. The strings are the nerves of a violin or a piano. But even without strings, the wind instruments emit a wonderful melody. Plants have no autonomic nervous system, without which processes of nutrition, respiration and metabolism of humans and higher animals are impossible, and yet all these processes occur in plants. "(Fechner)

If you turn the underside of a vine leaf to the light, it will bend and turn persistently to have its upper side in the light. Amazing are the instinctive movements of climbing plants. The plant first grows in height, and then it bends its stem horizontally and makes a circular movement, trying to find a support. The longer the stem grows, the bigger is the circle, that is, the plant is continuously searching. Finally, the stem can't carry its own weight, falls to the ground and crawls over it, looking for another support. Also in this case it is governed by a certain guideline. For example, a convolvulus never winds around inorganic or dead organic supports, but only around living plants, to which it adheres avidly because its own roots in the soil quickly die, and it drains the nutrients with the help of the special nipples out of the entwined plants.

Plants are known to sleep when the leaves bend or fold up, and the flowers hang their heads and close. Surprisingly expedient are the pistil's movement in certain plants to fertilize the stigma with pollen.

In the evening a lot of flowers in a meadow turn their heads to the sun, as if saying their evening prayer to it, and after sunset they sleep quietly till the next morning, turning to the east to meet the sun with their joyful morning prayer. The fragrance of flowers is their burning incense to God, and the flowers are the censers. Water-lilies open wide enjoying the light and air under the blue sky; they fold their petals and sink into the water when it gets dark.

There is no definite border between the worlds of plants and animals , because in protozoa there are many almost completely similar forms, of which some are the beginning of flora, the others of fauna, and it is almost impossible to find any difference between them. The simplest forms of animals, such as the river hydra, the volvulus, are quite similar to plants, and their vital functions are almost indistinguishable from one another. The class of protozoa is the starting point of the two magnificent worlds of creatures - plants and animals. The plant world in its gradual development has reached such magnificent, impressive forms as wonderfully fragrant flowers, slender palm trees and cypress trees, majestic cedars of Lebanon, mighty oaks and giant sequoias, which live for three thousand years. In comparison such primitive forms of animal life as polyps, sea cucumbers, starfish and worms are quite insignificant, and it would be strange to recognize the spirituality of these lower forms of animals, yet refuse to recognize the spirituality of highly perfect, and even grandiose, plant forms.

There is no doubt at all that the entire plant and animal world is endowed with at least the most basic of the gifts of the Holy Spirit, the spirit of life.

For the vast majority of naturalists, the "vitalists" and "neo-vitalists" doctrine of vital force is odious and absurd. But just think about the following facts.

According to the observations of Spalantsani, in swamps and in the sand of gutters live rotifers, gelatinous in the normal state. They can dry up while still remaining in the sand to such an extent that, if pressed with the end of the needle, they break like a grain of salt. However if in four years time the sand would be moistened, the dried rotifers would come to life again. They can withstand drying at 54° C, whereas in a living state, they die if the water temperature reaches 25° Celsius.

John Franklin in his first trip to the North American coast of the Arctic Ocean saw that fish, frozen immediately after they were dragged from the water, turned into a mass of ice so that they could be hacked to pieces with an axe, and that their frozen intestines were like solid ice chunks. However, some of such undamaged frozen fish came to life after they were defrosted near the fire. These facts indicated that, although every trace of life in the body had disappeared, yet the ability to come back to life might remain under favourable conditions, if only there were no changes in the anatomical or physiological spheres, which would have made impossible the retrieving of vital functions. It is known that wheat, barley and mustard found in Egyptian mummies, stored for 3000 years, if they had not been subjected to harmful effects damaging their enzymatic processes, give excellent germination when put in the favourable conditions of moisture and heat.

The next experiment was made by J. Becquerel in Paris in 1909. Seeds of wheat, alfalfa and white mustard were dried in vacuum for 6 months at 40°C and then sealed in vacuum in glass tubes. These tubes were sent to London and they were held there for three weeks in liquid air at about -190°C, and then another 77 hours in liquid hydrogen at -250°C. In Paris, the tube was opened again, and the seeds were put in a moist bath at 28°C. It was found that germination was completely normal. No difference was observed in comparison with samples of seeds stored in the usual way. At such a low temperature as -250°C, every trace of life is excluded. Even the most energetic chemical reactions wouldn't occur at such a low temperature.

These experiments show us that temporary death is possible if the action, inhibiting life functions, does not extend to the destruction of the body ("Degeneration of energies" by Svedberg).

If it is clear that the temporary death of seeds and animals does not prevent their coming to life once again, surely we have no right to say that all this is possible without some unknown but evident force, vital energy, not amenable to harmful agents that destroy the life of seeds and plants? And this energy can certainly be only a spiritual energy, the life-giving power of the Holy Spirit.

The above-mentioned amazing facts of life and spirituality of plants allow us to agree with Edward Hartmann when he argues that plants have an unconscious imagination and an unconscious will. Leibniz, in his turn, ascribes to monads a vague imagination and aspiration. A plant is a monad.

Our belief in the spirit in plants, of course, doesn't contradict at all the opinion of St. Anthony the Great on the impossibility of plants having a soul. Here are his words:

"I have written the present paragraph for the information of those who are simple, against men who assert that plants and grasses have a soul. Plants have physical life, but have no soul. Man is called a rational animal, because he is endowed with mind and capable of acquiring knowledge. Other animals – those on the ground and in the air who possess voice – breathe and have a soul. All things that grow and decrease can be called alive because they live and grow, but it cannot be said that all such things have soul. There are four kinds of living beings: some of them are immortal and have souls, such as angels; others have mind, soul and breath, such as men; yet others have soul and breath, such as animals; and others only have life, such as plants. Life in plants is maintained without soul or breathing, without mind or immortality. But all the rest, too, cannot be without life. Every human soul is very changeable." (Early Fathers from the Philokalia, tr. E.Kadloubovsky and G.Palmer, ed. Faber & Faber, 1973)

There is no contradiction of course. We do not ascribe a soul to plants in the same sense as we understand a human's and an animal's soul, but only like the unconscious imagination and the unconscious will.

Anthony the Great, speaking of the soul of animals, of course, was referring to the higher animals, and not to such as coelenterates, molluscs, sponges, even slipper animalcules, of whose existence or the question whether they belonged to the animal world or not he could have had no idea. Of course, these simplest animal forms, as to their spirituality, are not higher than plants, and might be even lower, and they are endowed with the spirit of life only, like any animal.

So, let us investigate thoroughly our knowledge of the spirit of the higher animals and humans.

Chapter 5. The Soul of Animal and the Soul of Man

According to physiologists' point of view, the activity of consciousness, that is, psychic activity should be seen as an enormously complex system of unconditioned and conditioned reflexes, initially formed and constantly re-formed, as a huge chain of perceptions, brought into the brain by receptors, analyzed by the brain to generate a motoric response.

Our brilliant scholar on higher nervous activity, I. P. Pavlov, defines consciousness as follows: "Consciousness seems to me as the nervous activity of a certain area of the cerebral hemispheres, which has an optimal (probably an average) excitability at a certain moment under certain conditions. At the same moment the rest of the cerebral hemispheres are in a state of more or less reduced excitability.

New reflexes are easily formed and differentiations are successfully worked out in the area of the cerebral hemispheres with optimal excitability. It is at that moment, so to speak, the creative department of the cerebral hemispheres. Other parts of the hemispheres with a reduced excitability are not able to do the same, and their functions in this case are mainly previously developed reflexes, arising stereotypically under appropriate stimuli.

The activity of the other parts is what we subjectively call the unconscious, automatic activity.

The part with the optimal activity is not, of course, a fixed one, on the contrary, it constantly moves around the cerebral hemispheres, depending on connections existing between the centres, and the area with reduced excitability varies under the influence of stimuli.

If we could see through the skull of a consciously thinking person, and if the part of the cerebral hemispheres with increased excitability could emit light, we would see an oddly shaped bright spot moving about the cerebral hemispheres, constantly changing in shape and size, surrounded by a more or less considerable shadow on all the rest of the hemispheres.

We fully accept this deep scientific understanding of the activities of consciousness, but we do not consider it complete. We are even prepared to subscribe to the basic thesis of materialism: "Being determines consciousness", but only under the condition that the term "being" signifies both material and spiritual realms.

In order to present our understanding of consciousness, we should divide it into acts, states and volumes of consciousness. Thought flows like a stream. Thought flashes like a bright light. Thought digs into the depths of existence.

Calm and deliberate volitional actions; sudden outbursts: stabbing the heart of the offender; the constant effort of will in the course of life, directed to achieving important plans and objectives; a quiet love, devoid of passion; profound, calm, aesthetic pleasure; the stormy passions of anger, and fear; deep constant devotion to God, which governs my entire life – these are acts of consciousness.

They are caused by: 1) perceptions of the sensors, 2) the organic sensations of our bodies, 3) the perceptions of our transcendental being, 4) the perceptions of the higher spiritual world, 5) the impacts of our spirit.

Acts of consciousness are not isolated: thought is always accompanied by feeling; feeling and will by thought, and feeling by volitional movements; acts of will are always associated with feelings and thoughts; the complex of these simultaneously occurring acts of consciousness determines the state of consciousness. These states of consciousness are constantly changing, for the acts of consciousness are in constant motion.

The volume of consciousness, also constantly changing, usually increasing, is determined by the richness, diversity and depth of acts and states of consciousness. Our spirit is always involved in the acts and states of consciousness, identifying and directing them. In its turn, the spirit grows and changes owing to the activity of consciousness, through its individual acts and states.

This is our idea of the full range of human psychic activity. But not only people have a soul, the animals have it as well. "The soul of the animal is in its blood." And an animal, like man, comprises the spirit, the soul and the body.

What is the soul? In its simplest kind, in animals, it might be the complex of organic and sensual perceptions, thoughts and feelings, traces of memory, united by self-awareness (the mind in higher types of animals), or only the complex of organic sensations (in the lower type of animals). The primitive spirit of the animals is just the breath of life (in the lower type of animals). When climbing the ladder in the hierarchy of creatures spirituality increases, and the breath of life is enriched with rudiments of the mind, will and emotions.

The human soul is much higher in its essence, for the spirit participating in its activities is incomparable with the spirit of animals. It may have the highest gifts of the Holy Spirit, which St. Isaiah the Prophet (11:1-3) calls the spirit of fear of God, the spirit of wisdom and understanding, the spirit of strength and might, the spirit of light, the spirit of reason, the Spirit of the Lord, or the gift of supreme piety and inspiration. The spirit and the soul of a man are inseparably connected in a single entity during his life, but people possess different degrees of spirituality. There are those whom the Apostle Paul calls "spiritual" (1Cor.2:15). As we have said, there may be people - beasts, people - plants, but on the other hand: people - angels. The first are not much different from the beasts, because their spirituality is very low, and the last ones are close to the bodiless spirits, who have neither body nor soul. So, the soul can be described as a combination of organic and sensual perceptions, traces of memories, thoughts, feelings, and acts of the will, in which the highest manifestations of the spirit are not obligatory, for they are not present in animals and in some people. The Apostle Jude spoke about them: "These are the ones who segregate themselves; they are animals, not having the Spirit." (Jude1:19)

The life of the spirit during the material life is closely intertwined with those psychic acts which are common to humans and animals, i.e. with organic sensations and the perceptions of the five senses; the latter, in turn, are inextricably connected with the life of the body, of the brain in particular; and they disappear at the death of the body. Therefore, the primitive soul of animals is mortal, as those elements of human consciousness are mortal, that have roots in the physical body (organic and sensory perceptions).

However those elements of self-consciousness that are associated with the life of the spirit are immortal. Immortal is the spirit, which, as we show below, may exist without any connection with the body and the soul. Materialists deny the immortality of the soul, precisely as they do not want to know anything about the spirit. But we acknowledge the mortality of that kind of self-consciousness which rests solely on a physiological basis.

Let us see now if the Scriptures give us reason to understand the spirit and the soul as we have just outlined. We believe that our understanding of the soul and the spirit is in perfect accordance with the Revelation.

The word "soul" is used in the Scriptures in various ways.

As in common parlance, it may simply mean the person: "Not any soul". "No soul of you shall perish," Saint Paul says to his companions on the ship.

"The soul that sins, the same shall die. " (Ezek. 18:20)
In other parts the soul is synonymous with life.
"For their bread is of their soul; it will not enter into the house of the Lord." (Hos. 9:4)
But a number of texts clearly refer to what one might call the "animal soul."
"For he has satisfied the empty soul, and he has satisfied the hungry soul with good things...
Their soul abhorred all food, and they drew near even to the gates of death." (Ps.106(107):9,18)
"And I will lead back Israel to his habitation. And he will pasture on Carmel and Bashan, and his soul will be satiated at mount Ephraim and Gilead.." (Jer. 50: 19)
"The soul that blesses shall be made fat. " (Prov. 11:25)
"The lazy one is willing and then not willing. But the soul of he who labors shall be made fat." (Prov. 13:4)
"a dissolute soul will go hungry." (Prov. 19:15)
"A sated soul will trample the honeycomb. And a hungry soul will accept even bitter in place of sweet." (Prov. 27:7)
"Listen very closely to me, and eat what is good, and then your soul will be delighted by a full measure." (Is. 55:2)
"And their soul will be like an irrigated garden, and they will no longer be hungry." (Jer. 31:12) (This is about earthly goods).
"Bread becomes abominable to him in his life, and, to his soul, the meat..." (Job 33:20)
"And I will inebriate the soul of the priests with fatness..." (Jer. 31:14)
Let those who are used to the concept of the immortality of the soul not be confused with our words about the immortality of the spirit. It isn't a novelty, for in most fragments of the Scriptures, when speaking of death, it is said that the spirit is leaving the body and not the soul.

"For just as the body without the spirit is dead, so also faith without works is dead." (James 2:26)

"Who knows if the spirit of the sons of Adam ascend upward, and if the spirit of the beasts descend downward?" (Eccles. 3:21)

"And in the Spirit, he preached to those who were in prison, going to those souls." (1 Pet. 3:19)

"...and to the spirits of the just made perfect." (Heb. 12:23)

"And her spirit returned, and she immediately rose up." (Luke 8:55)

"Into thine hand I commit my spirit." (Ps.30(31):6)

"Father, into your hands I commend my spirit." (Luke 23:46)

"Lord Jesus, receive my spirit." (Acts 7:59)

"His spirit will depart, and he will return to his earth. In that day, all their thoughts will perish." (Ps.145(146):4)

" and the dust returns to its earth, from which it was, and the spirit returns to God, who granted it." (Eccles. 12:7)

The last two quotes are particularly important to support our view that mortal are those elements of the soul that are associated with the life of the body, i.e. the five senses and thought processes, inextricably connected with the activity of the brain.

"...in that very day his thoughts perish... ", i.e. the activity of consciousness, which requires all the perceptions of the living brain, will stop.

Not a soul, but the spirit, goes forth and returneth to his earth, i.e. into eternity. Ashes will return to the earth as they were, but "the spirit shall return unto God who gave it."

And the spirit of an animal, of course, must be immortal because it also has its source in the Spirit of God, the immortal Spirit.

The idea of the immortality of the spirit of animals is clearly present in the famous words of Apostle Paul on the hope of all creation (Rom.8:20-21): "For the creature was made subject to emptiness, not willingly, but for the sake of the One who made it subject, unto hope.

For the creature itself shall also be delivered from the servitude of corruption, into the liberty of the glory of the sons of God." In a few places of the Scriptures death is defined as the departure of the soul (not the spirit) from the body (Gen. 35:18; Ps. 15:10). This is easily explained by the fact that in the Bible, and particularly in the Psalms, the word "soul" is often used in an conventional sense, i.e. as the sum of all mental and spiritual acts. But we say also that the spirit and the soul of man are combined in a single entity, which can be simply called the soul.

One should understand in this way the texts speaking about the soul of the Lord Jesus Christ.

"If he lays down his life because of sin.." (Is. 53:10)

"For he was neither left behind in Hell..." (Acts 2:31)

"My soul is sorrowful, even unto death." (Matt. 26:38)

"Now is my soul troubled." (John 12:27)

"Because his soul has labored, he will see and be satisfied." (Is. 53:11)

The Lord suffered and died in His human nature, and therefore we can understand these words. But the soul of God Himself is mentioned in the following texts:

"And my soul became contracted concerning them, just as their soul also varied concerning me."(Zech. 11:8)

"And he was touched by their miseries." (Judg. 10:16)

But, of course, it is only a metaphor. It is impossible to speak of the soul of the Spirit in absolute terms as of the human soul which is a limited, incarnate spirit. Here we can speak only about the analogy with the human spirit, according to which we ascribe the mind, thought, will and emotions to God. In this way we understand the image of God in every man.

We have already mentioned self-consciousness, self-awareness. How should we understand this? Man forms the consciousness of his own personality through organic sensations received from his body, through perceptions derived from his senses, through the entire set of memories, the understanding of his spirit, character and mood.

How is self-consciousness formed as the sum of those elements, and what is its subject ? It is not the mind, as is generally understood, but the spirit. For the mind is only a part of the spirit, and not the whole spirit. A part can't grasp the whole. This is an important conclusion to which we shall refer later when discussing immortality. And it is not arbitrary, but based on the words of Apostle Paul:

"And who can know the things that are of a man, except the spirit which is within that man? So also, no one knows the things which are of God, except the Spirit of God." (1 Cor. 2:11)

We learn the deepest essence of our being not by our mind, but by our spirit. Self-awareness is a function of the spirit, not of the mind. We learn about God's Grace granted to us by Him not by the spirit of this world, but by our spirit, given to us by God, too.

The same thought is in Solomon's words of Wisdom: "TThe spirit of a man is a lamp to the Lord, which investigates all the secrets of the inner self." (Prov. 20:27)

A lot can be found in the Scriptures on the Spirit as the supreme power of our spiritual activity. Here are some examples:

"For whatever a man will have sown, that also shall he reap. For whoever sows in his flesh, from the flesh he shall also reap corruption. But whoever sows in the Spirit, from the Spirit he shall reap eternal life." (Gal.6:8)

"So what is, at first, not spiritual, but animal, next becomes spiritual." (1 Cor. 15:46)

This means that spirituality is the highest achievement of the human soul.

"But the fruit of the Spirit is charity, joy, peace, patience, kindness, goodness, forbearance, meekness, faith, modesty, abstinence, chastity." (Gal. 5:22-23)

"...in spirit, fervent..." (Rom. 12:11)

"Yet by the Spirit, he speaks mysteries." (1 Cor. 14:2)

"But I see now that there is only breath in men, and that it is the inspiration of the Almighty that gives understanding." (Job 32: 8)

"Indeed, the spirit is willing, but the flesh is weak." (Matt. 26:41)

"And my words and preaching were not the persuasive words of human wisdom, but were a manifestation of the Spirit and of virtue," (1 Cor. 2:4)

"Cast all your transgressions, by which you have transgressed, away from you, and make for yourselves a new heart and a new spirit." (Ezek. 18:31)

Here is the idea of the close connection between the heart and the spirit, which confirms the primary role of the heart in consciousness as we mentioned earlier.

" And my spirit leaps for joy in God my Savior." (Luke 1:47)

The human spirit rejoices in God, worships God, seeks God and comes closer to God. And this, of course, is the highest ability of a man's soul.

Of course, this most perfect manifestation of the spirituality of the human soul can be only a gift of the Holy Spirit. This is quite clearly demonstrated in Revelation:

" And I will place my Spirit in your midst. " (Ezek. 36:27)

" Therefore, because you are sons, God has sent the Spirit of his Son into your hearts, crying out: "Abba, Father.""(Gal. 4:6)

"For God has not given us a spirit of fear, but of virtue, and of love, and of self-restraint." (2 Tim.1:7)

"But God has revealed these things to us through his Spirit. For the Spirit searches all things, even the depths of God." (1 Cor.2:10)

"Certainly, to one, through the Spirit, is given words of wisdom; but to another, according to the same Spirit, words of knowledge; to another, in the same Spirit, faith; to another, in the one Spirit, the gift of healing;" (1 Cor.12:8-9)

"In him, you also have been built together into a habitation of God in the Spirit." (Eph.2:22)

"And I will give to you a new heart, and I will place in you a new spirit. And I will take away the heart of stone from your body, and I will give to you a heart of flesh. And I will place my Spirit in your midst. And I will act so that you may walk in my precepts and keep my judgments, and so that you may fulfill them." (Ezek.36:26-27)

"The Lord...forming the spirit of man within him..." (Zech.12:1)

"...what is born of the Spirit is spirit." (John 3:6)

"For God does not give the Spirit by measure." (John 3:34)

"...he has given to us from his Spirit." (1 John 4:13)

"...if anyone does not have the Spirit of Christ, he does not belong to him." (Rom. 8:9)

"But we have not received the spirit of this world, but the Spirit who is of God..." (1 Cor. 2:12)

The descent of the Holy Spirit upon the apostles really confirmed the truth, which is stated by all of these texts: the human spirit has its source in the Spirit of God.

All who are familiar with the Scriptures know how many texts in the Old and the New Testament are about the devil and unclean spirits and the evil effect of them on the human spirit. St. John the Evangelist in his first epistle (1 John 2:22) speaks directly of the spirit of Antichrist. The influence of this spirit, hostile to the spirit of God, on the human heart is huge. Defining above what are the sources for the acts of consciousness, we talked about the perceptions of the higher spiritual world. In this case we are referring to effects of the Spirit of God and the spirit of Satan on the human spirit.

Whence and how was the spirit of Satan born?

Pride is the antithesis of humility, rage and hatred are the antithesis of love, blasphemy is the antithesis of love for God, vanity and greed are the antithesis of love for people. The negative occurs and is growing steadily at the cost of the positive. Darkness appears by the loss of light, cold appears by the loss of warmth, motionlessness and stagnation appear by the loss of movement. The spirit of Satan was born out of the loss of love for God.

The Spirit of God and the spirit of Satan are everywhere and influence all living beings. Something that lives is capable of perceiving one akin to it. Animals take in oxygen and plants take in carbon dioxide from the air. There are beings that do not require light and avoid it. Some bacteria (called anaerobes) can live only in the absence of oxygen and they die in the air. People who are akin in spirit to Satan, perceive that spirit and are steadily developing in it. Paul the Apostle says about it in images: "To the one we are the savour of death unto death; and to the other the savour of life unto life. And who is sufficient for these things?" (2 Cor. 2:16)

People who are akin in their spirit to God-Love, receive the Holy Spirit and are steadily improving in goodness and love. Jesus Christ Himself and the Prophet Ezekiel testify to the spiritual influences from outside on the human spirit:

"The Spirit inspires where he wills. And you hear his voice, but you do not know where he comes from, or where he is going." (John 3:8)

"It is the Spirit who gives life. The flesh does not offer anything of benefit. The words that I speak unto you, they are spirit, and they are life..." (John 6:64)

"And after this was spoken to me, the Spirit entered into me, and he set me on my feet. And I heard him speaking to me..." (Ezek. 2:2)

The spirit came from outside into the man who has a soul. The same is said by the Apostles:

"...Paul stood firm in the Word, testifying to the Jews that Jesus is the Christ." (Acts 18:5)

"And now, behold, being obliged in spirit, I am going to Jerusalem..." (Acts 20:22)

Through God's work the spirit of one person can be transferred to another.

"The spirit of Elijah has rested upon Elisha." (2 Kin. 2:15)

"And I will take from your spirit, and I will deliver it to them..." (Num. 11:17)

What should we say about the spirit of animals?

They, like people, are carriers of a certain spirit according to their nature. In one breed there may be a bold and a cowardly animal, an evil and a moody one, an affectionate and a funny one. They do not possess the higher forms of spirituality, religiosity, moral sense, philosophical and scientific thinking, fine art and musical sensitivity. But love and the beginnings of altruism, and aesthetic sense are inherent in animals too. Not the highest form of love, not Divine love, but only love for family, in which swans and doves are, perhaps, even superior to men. Suicide is known among swans having lost their female: they fly high up, fold their wings and drop like a stone on the ground.

The lower on the ladder of perfection of zoological forms animals are, the lower degree of spirituality they have. The exception to this rule is love among birds. We can to some extent put this in parallel with the fact that the highest form of love and religion are often found among simple, uneducated people. Higher animals, having spirituality, even a limited one, must have self-awareness in a primitive form. Couldn't a dog express, "I am cold, I am sick, my master treats me badly"? The degree of consciousness in animals is determined by the development of their mind and the degree of spirituality available to them.

Chapter 6. The Spirit is not indubitably connected with the Body and the Soul

What is the relationship between the spirit, the soul and the body? The materialists who do not recognize the spirit as real, reduce all manifestations of the psyche to processes occurring in the brain, and above all, in the cortical substance of its hemispheres, and all psychic acts are considered to be functions of the brain. To a large extent this is true. Physiologists have determined precisely the dependence of psychic acts and states on normal or pathological functions of the nervous system in general, and especially the brain, and consequently, on functions of the body, on internal secretion, on the entire complex hormonal system that has a powerful influence on the brain and nerves.

Everything that happens in an organism, and even its anatomical structure, causes a deep imprint on the psyche. Various structures of the body correspond to some form of character, and the character is one of the most important manifestations of the soul and the spirit.

But can we say that a purely materialistic concept of the psyche is quite justified in those undoubted physiological data? By no means!

After all, the same physiology, and especially the great discoveries of Pavlov and his school, found that the central nervous system predominates over all the somatic processes, it determines and directs the work of all organs, their growth and trophic state; it influences powerfully the course of physiological processes. But the nervous system is the organ of the psyche; according to concepts of vulgar materialism, even thoughts and feelings were treated as the secretions of the brain. This primitive idea was left behind a long time ago, but the modern materialists attribute the psychic functions to the brain.

And if so, along with the lower functions there should be included the higher ones too, which dominate all lower functions, and inseparable from them in the same manner as the function of contraction can't be separated from the muscle tissue. Therefore, we may consider all the impacts of the central nervous system on organs and tissues as psychic impacts. And if there is no doubt that somatic processes largely determine the course of mental processes, it is equally certain and should be recognized that there is a psychological impact on all somatic processes.

The powerful influence of the psyche of a patient on the course of his illness is well known. The patient's state of mind, his trust or distrust of the doctor, the depth of his faith and hope for healing or, conversely, mental depression, caused by careless doctors talking about the seriousness of his illness in his presence, determine to a great extent the outcome. Psychotherapy, which consists in the doctors' verbal, or rather spiritual impact on the patient, is a widely recognized method of treating many diseases, often giving excellent results.

Charles Richet explains the true miracles at Lourdes by the powerful influence of the brain (we would say the spirit). Of the three miracles which he takes as examples, the most wonderful one is the healing of Derruder, a worker who in 1875 had an open fracture of the tibia complicated by infection. There was a heavy suppuration, the bones had not knitted, and the lower part of his shinbone with the foot was dangling loose. Eight years later he went on a pilgrimage to the holy city of Lourdes to pray for his recovery, and there he was suddenly healed. He could stand and walk, using both legs while for eight years he could only walk with crutches.

No less surprising is the other case. In 1897 a person called Gargam had a fractured spine in a train accident, with as result paralysis of both legs with muscle atrophy and incipient gangrene. In Lourdes, Gargam was cured almost instantly: having just entered the cave, he was able to take a few shaky steps. The next day the festering sores of his foot were healed. He could walk without a stick, in spite of the atrophy of muscles. Three weeks later, he had gained 10 kg in weight and was able to return to work.

We could cite many similar examples of healing at the opening of the relics of St. Seraphim of Sarov, from the hagiography of St. Pitirim of Tambov, and many other saints.

We cannot agree with the opinion of C. Richet that these surprising facts are only physiological impacts of the brain, albeit powerful ones. It is impossible because all of the brain processes and all the impacts of the brain take time, and these miraculous healings have occurred almost beyond time, in a fraction of an instance. Such speed of action is possible only for the spirit. In addition, Gargam had a severe spinal cord injury, as evidenced not only by paralysis of the legs and muscle atrophy, but by incipient gangrene. According to our medical knowledge all these were irreversible changes, and no physiological impact of the brain, even the most powerful one, could possibly have reversed them.

With this chapter we substantiate our statement in the third chapter that the spirit creates forms. The assertion that the spiritual is determined by the material is narrow-minded and unreasonable, because we must admit that there is a reverse effect of spiritual influence on the matter of the body through the nervous system, the organ of psyche. The Spirit not only creates the forms of material bodies, directing and defining the process of growth, but it can take these forms directly, through materialization.

No matter how we feel about spiritualism, some facts certainly can't be denied. Only those who judge the spiritualistic phenomena offhand, can lightly and indiscriminately deny them. Everyone who has read the extensive chapter on this subject in C. Richet's "The Treatise on Metaphysics," will be convinced of the reality of facts of materialization of the spirit in some unknown, special forms of matter.

I must however, give a few examples of materializations from the great number of them. When witnessing them even the most stubborn sceptics, prominent scientists, regretted their mistrust.

While Sir William Crookes was experimenting with the famous medium Home during daylight, he saw a graceful hand rising up from the table and giving him a flower. "It appeared and disappeared three times, giving me the opportunity to make sure it was as real as my own hand, and all that time I was firmly holding the medium's hands and feet. The hand and fingers did not always seem to me dense and just alive. Sometimes they seemed the coagulation of a cloud of steam; a white cloud, as it seemed, was forming and transforming itself into a perfect hand. It seemed like human flesh, like the hands of those present. Around its wrist and shoulder it became like steam and was lost in a cloud of light. I tried to hold the hand in my hand firmly, determined not to let it disappear, but it released itself without even the slightest effort, and turned into steam."

Richet obtained copies of such fluid hands. The ghost dipped its hands into paraffin molten at 43°C. When the hand came out it left a paraffin mould and disappeared. The mould was filled with gypsum and the paraffin was removed. On the photograph of this plaster cast the smallest details of the skin, the lacework of veins can be seen. To avoid any possibility of the medium exchanging the cast cholesterol was secretly added to the paraffin. Cholesterol becomes a purple colour when sulphuric acid is added, and a piece torn off the cast had indeed become purple when the sulphuric acid was added. The hands and feet of the medium were tightly held during all the experiments.

For all those who believe that the Holy Scriptures are all truth, there can be no doubt about the ability to materialize the spirit, because they know that the Medium of Endor evoked the spirit of the Prophet Samuel on request of king Saul "And the king said to her: "Do not be afraid. What have you seen?" And the woman said to Saul, "I saw gods ascending from the earth."

And he said to her, "What appearance does he have?" And she said, "An old man ascends, and he is clothed in a cloak." And Saul understood that it was Samuel. And he bowed himself upon his face on the ground, and he reverenced.

Then Samuel said to Saul, "Why have you disquieted me, so that I would be raised up?"" (1 Sam. 28:13-15)

If the facts of evoking the dead, that is, materialization of the spirit, were not generally known in antiquity, then why would Moses forbid contact with those evoking the dead, saying "Do not turn aside to astrologers, nor consult with soothsayers, so as to be polluted through them." (Lev.19:31).

"Do not let there be found among you one who practices the occult, nor one who uses spells, nor one who consults demonic spirits, nor a diviner, nor one who seeks the truth from the dead." (Deut. 18:10-11)

Is it possible that Isaiah, the great prophet would say meaningless words? And he said: "And they will seek answers from their false images, and their diviners, and those led by demons, and their seers." (Is.19:3) How explain the appearing of Moses and Elijah to the Lord Jesus Christ at His Transfiguration on Mount Tabor, if not as the materialization of the spirit? And what about the appearing of angels in human form? An angel had appeared to Gideon and his wife, and then disappeared in the smoke of burning meat and broth in the same way as the materialized spirits disappear when conjured up by spiritualists (see Judg. 6:19–21; 13:20).

During the First World War, a professor of physics, N., a materialist, was staying for a while in a Ukrainian village in summer. In the evening he came out onto the porch when the owner of the hut went to the gate to bring her cow in. Suddenly she seemed stunned, clasped her hands, exclaimed, "Peter!" and fainted. Later, she told the professor that she saw her son, who was at war, smiling and joyful. That day he was killed.

The appearance of ghosts at the moment of a person's death is a well-known and indisputable fact. Richet gives many examples of this kind in his book. I will mention only a few of them.

1. Colonel N. was sleeping in his room in London. At dawn, he suddenly woke up and saw Pool, his comrade in the army, in a khaki uniform and a helmet on his head, with a thick black beard, which he hadn't had when N. knew him.

N. knew that Pool was in the Transvaal, on the front. The vision was so clear that N. almost mistook it for the reality: he saw the face, the lively eyes, the khaki uniform, the helmet. N. sat on the bed, staring at Pool who spoke to him: "I was killed by a stab wound in the chest" and saying this, he slowly raised his hand to his chest. "The General ordered me to go."

N. spoke about this appearance to some of his comrades and the next day he got news that Pool was killed in battle. He wore a khaki uniform and a beard, and he was killed by a stab-wound in the chest.

2. Once at night a man called Panchi, who lived in Pisa saw his father, pale and dying, pronouncing the words: "Kiss me one last time, because I'm leaving forever", and he felt the cold touch of lips to his. Although there was no any other, common reason to suspect any misfortune, he went to Florence and

there he heard that his father had died last night at the hour when he had had the vision of the ghost.

A similar case took place in my family. My sister died in a wing of the house, where our elder brother lived. He dozed off while sitting on the couch, and awoke at one o"clock at night, feeling clearly a breeze in front of his face and a kiss on his cheek. At this moment our sister breathed her last.

3. Dr. Marie de Thiele, who lived in Lausanne, heard a knock at the door at 6 o'clock in the morning. Someone came in, wearing a black dress, and wrapped in a white translucent fabric like in a veil. The cat in the room arched her back, her fur bristling, growling terribly and shaking. After some time, Madame de Thiele got to know that one of her best friends, whom however, she hadn't thought of at the time of the appearance had died of acute peritonitis in India.

Here's another example of this kind. Miss C. was stroking her cat which was lying on her lap. Suddenly the cat jumped up in horror, arched her back with her fur bristling, and began hissing frantically. Then Miss C. saw an old woman with a pale face sitting in a chair near her and staring at her. The cat rushed like mad with a tumultuous leap through the door. Miss C. cried out for help in terror. Her mother entered the room, and the ghost disappeared. Miss C. had the vision for about five minutes. She was told later that an old woman had hanged herself in that room.

Richet gives many vivid examples of the collective seeing of ghosts. Here is just one of them.

In 1896 Mrs Teleshov was in her living room in St. Petersburg with her five children and the dog Mustash. Suddenly the dog began barking loudly, and everyone saw a little boy of six wearing a shirt. They recognized Andrew, a son of the milkman, who they knew was sick. The ghost came out of the oven, went over the heads of those present and disappeared through the open window. It lasted for about five seconds.

Mustash did not stop barking and chasing the moving phantom. At that moment little Andrew breathed his last.

Here's how Richet qualifies seeing ghosts: it is impossible to think that these images, the noise, these ghosts, sometimes having been seen by a group of people, do not represent an objective reality (mechanically objective). And yet we can't prove it absolutely and unquestionably.

It is just the same with all knowledge based on observations. If it were impossible to explain the phenomena of those materialized objects otherwise than by collective hallucinations, then due to the strangeness of these phenomena we should consider them unreal. However, experimental data of the materializations are quite convincing. Ghosts can be observed. This observation can't be exactly as in the [common scientific. Translator] experimental methods, for no photographic plates, no microphone, no weights, no galvanometer can be used by those watching. The only real evidence of the materialization, which is material and luminous, may be its simultaneous perception by several persons, and, moreover, exactly in the same way. If two normal, reasonable people describe exactly the same vision, exclaim simultaneously, inform each other of their experiences in the presence of the phantom, it would be absurd to think of a completely identical hallucination of both of them.

Somewhat different from the appearance of ghosts, but very close to it is the dead calling the living, seen in the form of ghosts only by those whom they call and invisible to everyone else. In other cases these calls are perceived as a voice, without the appearance of ghosts. Facts of this kind are extremely numerous and undoubtedly trustworthy.

Here are a few striking examples.

1. The case reported by Bozzano refers to Ray, a child 2 years and 7 months old. His brother of eight months had just died. His ghost appeared regularly to little Ray, who often saw his

dead little brother sitting on a chair and beckoning to him. He said, "Mum, Ray's little brother is calling him, he wants Ray there with him." On another occasion he said, "Do not cry, mother, little brother is smiling. Ray will go to him". Ray, wise for his age, died two months and seven days after his brother. This case is even more surprising, for children at such an early age do not understand what death is.

2. Louise C. 45 years old died after laparotomy. During her illness she had always asked that her three-year-old niece Lily, whom she loved, should be brought to her village after her recovery. Little Lily was very smart, very healthy; a month after the death of her aunt she would often suddenly interrupt her game, go to a window and stare somewhere. Her mother asked what she was looking at. "Aunt Louise is holding out her hands to me and calling me." Frightened, the mother tried to entertain her, but the child, not paying attention to her, took a chair to the window and for a few minutes did not take her eyes off the ghost of her aunt, visible to her only and calling her. She asked her sister, "How is it you can't see Tata? ("Tata" was a name their aunt was called in childhood and by her relatives). But her sister saw nothing. The visions stopped a few months later. On the 20th May little Lily became ill. Lying in bed and staring at the ceiling, she said that she saw her aunt, surrounded by little angels. "How beautiful it is, Mum," she said. Day by day she grew worse and worse, but she kept repeating, "This is my aunt. She has come to take me and she is holding out her hands to me." And she said to her weeping mother, "Do not cry, Mum, that's fine, the angels are around me." She died on the 3rd July 1896, four months after Louise.

3. The dead father of Philaret, the Metropolitan of Moscow, appeared to him in his sleep three months before his death and he said, "Remember the nineteenth." He died on the 19th November.

4. Mrs. Morrison, lying in bed in India, suddenly heard a voice: "When darkness comes, death will come." She sat up in bed frightened. The same voice slowly repeated the same words. Two days later her daughter became seriously ill. During that week there had not been a cloud in the sky, but on the eighth day there was suddenly a terrible storm. A few minutes before eleven o"clock the house was completely dark. Her little daughter died at 1 p.m..

The so-called externalization of living people is close to the phenomenon of ghosts of dead people. Examples may be found in the lives of many saints. In the Roman-Catholic hagiology the case of Alphonsus Liguori is well-known. On the 17th September 1774 he became motionless and silent in his cell. He didn't eat and spoke to no one. Then on the 22nd September in the morning he woke up and told his brethren that he had been with the Pope, who had just died. That same night 21st to 22nd September Pope Clement XIV died, and Alphonsus Liguori was beside him.

We can mention the case of externalization of Ambrose the Elder of Optina, our contemporary (died 1891). Avdotya, a peasant, who suffered from bad legs, went on foot to the Optina Monastery, expecting to be healed by Elder Ambrose. Seven miles from the monastery, she lost her way and in tears she fell on the ground. Soon she was approached by an old man in a cassock and cap who asked her why she was crying. The old man showed her the way to the monastery with his crutch. When she reached the hermitage where Ambrose lived she wormed her way in the crowd of women waiting to see the Elder. In a few minutes Fr. Ambrose's cell-monk came onto the porch and said loudly: "Where is Avdotya from Voronezh?" Avdotya was so astonished that she only reacted when the cell monk called a second time. Fifteen minutes later she came out in tears from the Elder in whom she had immediately recognized that very old man who had pointed out the path to the hermitage in the woods. Ambrose had very poor health, would leave his cell only in summer, and he would often fall asleep, always lying on the couch. Neither in the hermitage nor in the monastery there was anybody who looked like him. He had a striking appearance and Avdotya could not be mistaken.

Exteriorization of the human spirit often takes place in a hypnotic sleep.

Dr. Pierre Janet, while in Le Havre, put Leonie B. in a hypnotic sleep and suggested that she should go (in this hypnotic sleep) to Paris, to his apartment. After this suggestion Leonie suddenly stirred and cried: "Fire, fire"! Dr. Janet tried to calm her down. She woke up and then fell asleep again and woke up with the words: "Janet, I assure you that there is a fire in your apartment". Indeed, that day fire destroyed the Paris laboratory of Dr. Janet.

Let's remember how St. Basil the Blessed at the feast of Ivan the Terrible three times poured the cup of wine poured for him onto the floor, and replied to the angry shouting tsar, "I am putting out the fire in Novgorod." Indeed, at that same time a terrible fire raged in Novgorod!

What is so incredible then about the fact that the enlightened spirit of the saints always possess fully the transcendental powers which ordinary people manifest only in a state of somnambulism ? We can draw extremely important conclusions from these mysterious and utterly inexplicable facts. They are inexplicable not only in the present state of science, but are unlikely ever to be explained by psychic-physiological methods. These phenomena are, of course, of a very special order, radically different from those that are available to science. These are not psychic-physiological effects, but the effects of the spirit, temporarily or permanently separated from the body.

Exteriorization of the spirit of the living in the normal state (Ambrose the Elder) or under hypnosis (Leonei B.), of course, differs from the appearance of the dead in the form of materialized ghosts or mysterious voices predicting death or misfortune. But for all their differences, these unexplained phenomena suggest that the relationship between the spirit and the body is not unconditional, and that the spirit can exist separate from the body.

The appearances of the dead are, however, very important, even conclusive, proof of the existence of the spirit. The fact that the spirit can exist separately from the body may also be proved by the transfer of inherited spiritual qualities of parents to children. I'm talking about the inheritance of spiritual traits, because only the basic traits, their moral direction, their tendency to good or evil, the higher abilities of the mind, emotions and will are inherited, but the memories of parents' lives, their sensory or organic perceptions, their private thoughts and feelings connected rather with their heart than with their spirit, could never be inherited. This indicates a separation of the spirit from the body and the soul. The facts of heredity of the spirit are known and undeniable. In the twenties of the last century in America there lived a very corrupt young woman. She had already been sentenced to the gallows in her early youth but she escaped punishment through marrying and she had many children. After sixty years the number of her direct descendants had reached eighty. Of these, twenty were condemned for crimes, and the remaining sixty were drunks, lunatics, idiots, and paupers.

In a French family, called Lemoine, known in the history of the end of the XVIIth century, the hereditary transmission of the noblest qualities was noticeable. This is one of those families where the members are born, it seems, only for justice and mercy, in which virtue is transmitted by blood, supported by advice and is stimulated by great examples. (Flechet)

The history of the ancient Roman imperial families, the Spanish and French royal families shows many clear well-known examples of moral and mental degeneration.

Chapter 7. Transcendental spiritual Abilities

The Lord Jesus Christ came into the house of Jairus, to resurrect his dead daughter. He was pressed by the crowd. A woman having an incurable bleeding secretly touched him in the firm hope that she would be healed. Her blood flow immediately stopped. The Lord Jesus stopped too and asked, "Who touched me?" His disciples were surprised with this question: "Teacher, the crowd hems you in and presses upon you, and yet you say, 'Who touched me?" Jesus' response was amazing, "Someone has touched me. For I know that power has gone out from me." (Luke 8:46) Let's compare another fact to this one.

In the surgical clinic of Leipzig dr. Hansen made the following experiment in the presence of many professors. He asked dr. Hermann to turn his back to him, facing the wall, so that he could not see what dr. Hansen was going to do. After dr. Hermann did so, dr. Hansen put his right hand onto dr. Hermann's head while with his left hand he took a steel pen, dipped it into ink and touched his own tongue with it. At the same moment dr. Hermann felt the taste of ink in his mouth, which remained for an hour and was impossible to get rid of with any food.

The holy apostles passed on the grace of the priesthood by the laying-on of hands on the ordained heads. They healed the sick by the laying-on of hands. And now the sacrament of the priesthood is given by the episcopal laying-on of hands.

What has happened and is happening in all these cases? We are very far from being able to explain these striking facts; it is a matter for the future, if it is possible at all. But the facts are indisputable. Observations of mediums, who were in a trance (this so-called state like the most deep hypnotic sleep), but sometimes even in their normal condition, definitely established that a part of the motive power of the medium comes free, i.e. exteriorizes, is separated from him. This phenomenon of exteriorization explains the amazing spiritualist phenomena of movement, even different objects flying about, knocking, self-propelled automatic writing by pen or pencil. Suggestion in hypnosis or in the awakened state can be explained only by the exteriorization of the hypnotist's thought and its reception by the person who is being hypnotized.

After a séance where heavy objects have been moved about, the medium feels great fatigue, because muscle power has gone out of him.

The Lord Jesus Christ felt that virtue was going out of Him, healing the bleeding woman. These are facts of the same order, which surpass the scope of physiological phenomena: these are facts of a transcendental order.

There are many striking facts where we have to admit that, apparently, acting agents are the simultaneous exteriorization of thought and motive power and their telepathic transfer. I will limit myself to citing two examples:

1. At 7 A.M. Mrs Severi jumped out of bed, suddenly awakened by a strong blow to her face. She felt that her upper lip was split and put her handkerchief to stop the bleeding. But to her surprise, there was no blood on the cloth. As it became clear later, at the same very moment her husband, who had taken the boat early in the morning around the lake, was surprised by a sudden strong gust of wind. The rudder shot out of his hands and split his upper lip. He lost a lot of blood.

2. In 1848 in India, Mrs. Richardson saw in a dream that her husband, a general, who was fighting in a battle about 150 miles away, fell badly wounded, and she heard his voice: "Take this ring off my finger and send it to my wife." At about this hour (11 P.M.), the general, very badly wounded, transferred the command to major Lloyd and said, "Take this ring

off my finger and send it to my wife." The general survived his injury and recovered.

We know from the lives of many saints, that they knew the names of people whom they were meeting for the first time. Basil the Great recognized immediately through his enlightened spirit that St. Ephraim of Syria was entering the church, and he sent a deacon to call him by name. He had never seen Ephraim before. Through his spirit he knew that in the secret room of the house of the holy presbyter there was a man with a repulsive disease, of whom the presbyter has been selflessly taking care. He called the patient by his name.

We might consider it a legend. But what about a case that struck C. Richet?

Working at the Hotel-Dieu, he hypnotized a recovering girl. Once his friend, an American student who had never been to the hospital before, went to the Hotel-Dieu with him. Richet asked the sleeping girl, "Do you know the name of my friend?" She began to laugh. "Would you tell us the first letter of his name?" She replied, "N, then E; I don't know the third one, and the fourth letter is K". The student's name was Neak. Wasn't this the transcendental power of the human spirit? Who can explain it by physiological reasons?

Hypnotizing Leonie V., Dr. P. Janet once asked her "What happened to my friend N.?" Quickly, not even polite, she replied: "He burned his paw. Why was he so careless to overturn something?" "When did he overturn what?" "A red liquid in a small vial. His skin swelled immediately." Janet writes, "As I heard later, it was quite accurate as two hours before, the head of Janet's laboratory called N. Langua, preparing an alkaline solution of bromine, overturned the vessel with this solution of a red colour. He burned his hand, and blisters soon formed on the skin."

A deacon's wife came to Sarov from Penza to see St. Seraphim. She was standing at the back of the crowd waiting for her turn. Suddenly St. Seraphim, leaving the others, called her "Evdokia, come here quickly." Astonished by the fact that St. Seraphim, never having seen her, called her by her name, Evdokia approached. "Go back home quickly, or you will not find your son." Evdokia hurried back to Penza and she found her son, who had graduated cum laude from the seminary and obtained a post at the Kiev Academy, on the point of leaving, as he was afraid of arriving late.

Is there any difference between this case and Leonie B.'s clairvoyance and the misfortune of J. N. Langua?

What is so incredible about the fact that the enlightened spirit of the saints always have in full the transcendental abilities that some ordinary people manifest only in a state of somnambulism?

We possess more than the common five senses. We have an ability of perception of a higher order, unknown to physiologists. Charles Du Pröll in his book "The Philosophy of Mysticism" mentions such a remarkable fact. In 1845 Berzelius, a famous chemist, Reichenbach, a physicist, and Hochberger, a physician at a mineral water resort, conducted a highly interesting experiment. They spread out a set of chemicals wrapped in paper on a table before one of the so-called sensitive girls, called von Sakkendorf. She was asked to touch them with the palm of her right hand; after doing so, she reacted differently to the chemicals: some of them did not have any effect on her, but some caused a peculiar trembling in her hand. Then she was asked to sort them out and put in one group the substances which didn't have any influence on her and all the others in another.

Reichenbach says, "The founder of the electrochemical system Berzelius expressed considerable amazement when one group of the substances were without exception electropositive, and the other had a solely electronegative character: not a single electropositive chemical was among the electronegative ones and vice versa... Thus, the electrochemical classification of the chemicals, the building of which took centuries of labour and ingenuity was produced in 10 minutes by a simple girl, endowed with the talent of sensitivity just by touching them with her hand without special devices."

It is very likely that physics and physiology in the future will find an explanation for this special sensitivity. But it is important for us that this ability to distinguish the electrical properties of substances does not belong to all people, but only to a very few, who are called "sensitive". This term, of course, explains nothing, it just marks the extraordinary sensitivity in a certain field. We shall speak of it later.

Completely incomprehensible and even more extraordinary is the ability, found only among the most powerful mediums, to learn a lot about people by touching objects belonging to them. An example of such clairvoyance is given in the third chapter. Touching a tie wrapped in paper a somnambulist found out that a murderer in jail had hanged himself with it. Mrs Pieper, one of the best mediums, showed this ability more than once. Mrs X. gave her three strands of hair, marked with the letters "A", "B" and "C". She herself knew only the origin of strand C. Mrs Pieper said about strand A, "This is from Frode Smoggins. Who is this Smoggins?" Indeed, a person called M. had cut this strand off Mrs Smoggins and handed it to X. Mrs Pieper said about strand B, "This is a very sick person." The woman, whom this strand belonged to, died in the same year. She said about strand "C", "She takes great care of her hair." Mrs X. had secretly cut her mother's hair. "This is your mother. She has four children, two boys and two girls." All this was true.

Widely known are facts of creativity in dreams. Condorcet, Franklin, Michelet, Kandilyak, Arago give evidence of it. Voltaire imagined a big part of his "La Henriade" in his sleep, while La Fontaine created during his sleep the fable "The two doves." Maignan discovered two important theorems during his sleep.

Burdach says, "Often such important scientific ideas were born in my dream that I would suddenly wake up. In many cases they were dealing with subjects, with which I was busy at that time, and they were quite new in their content."

Coleridge fell asleep reading and woke up feeling that he had created two or three hundred verses, ready to be noted down. He wrote down fifty-four verses freely and as quickly as the pen could keep pace. But someone came to see him about some business or other and stayed for about an hour. And Coleridge, to his great chagrin, felt that he had only had a vague recollection of his vision, and only eight or ten verses remained in his memory, and all the rest had gone forever.

De Rossi used to lay a paper and pencil beside his bed. Waking suddenly he would note down the important thoughts that had come to him in a dream.

A very important subconscious activity may take place in reality and in a state on the border between sleep and wakefulness. What is called inspiration, very often comes in a state of more or less total eclipse of the consciousness of reality.

Théophile Gauthier said of Balzac, "He was like a frenzied somnambulist sleeping with open eyes. Immersed in deep meditation, he did not hear what was said." Hegel was calmly finishing his "Phenomenology of Spirit" in Jena, on the 4th October 1806, not realizing that the battle was raging around him. Beethoven, in the throes of inspiration, once appeared half naked in the street of Neustadt. He was taken to jail as a vagrant, and in spite of his indignation, no one believed that he was Beethoven. Schopenhauer said about himself, "My philosophical tenets appeared [in my mind] by themselves without my interference at moments when my will was as if asleep, and my mind was not focused on a predetermined direction... My personality was as if astranged to my work..."

Sometimes the subconscious movement is so clear that it seems a suggestion from outside. This is expressed in Musset's verse:

I do not work, I am listening, waiting...
As if someone unknown speaks into my ear...

Similar examples of Socrates (his daemon), Pascal, and Mozart have become classic.

Prophetic dreams may be called the supernatural abilities of the spirit, inexplicable by modern science. Here are two examples.

1. In 1885 in St. Petersburg a certain Lukaevsky, one of the top officials at the Ministry of Naval Affairs (which, however, does not mean that he often sailed at sea), dreamed that he was on board of a large ship, which collided with another ship; and he fell into the water along with other passengers and was drowning. After this dream, he was convinced he would die in a shipwreck, and in anticipation of imminent death he put his affairs in order. A few months later, when the memory of this dream had already faded, he received orders to go to one of the ports of the Black Sea. He remembered his dream, and on departure he said to his wife, "You will not see me anymore. When I die, put on mourning, but not that black veil, which I hate." Two weeks later the ship "Vladimir" by which Lukaevsky sailed collided with another ship, and Lukaevsky was drowned. Hanicke, one of the "Vladimir"'s passengers who was rescued, said that he was holding onto the same lifebelt with Lukaevsky for a few moments.

2. An intelligent Uzbek K., a former prominent member of the Tashkent city council, told me about an unusual occasion in his life.

A year after his father's death he dreamed that he was riding a horse across a deserted and hilly place. On one of the hills he saw his sister, who had died long ago. She angrily asked him why he never prayed for their father. Saying this she took him to a deep black pit, pushed him into it and said that he would stay in it for forty days. Shortly after this dream K. was arrested and taken to jail. During the interrogation, the police officer showed him two letters with his signature, which were addressed to the Emir of Bukhara. One of the letters contained K.'s appeal to the Emir to rise against the authority of the Russians and the other one contained the detailed plan of the rising. K. admitted that the signatures were indeed similar to his, but that he never wrote these letters or signed them. However he could do nothing to prove his statement, and it was clear that he would be hanged. In despair, he prayed to God for salvation, and, remembering his dream, he began praying for the repose of his father's soul. So about a month passed. One day while praying he fell asleep and he heard a voice in his dream saying, "Write your signature on three separate sheets of paper, put them together, one on top of the other, and look through them under the lamp." When K. woke up, he did as he was told and he found that his signatures were not identical. He repeated this experiment many times, and he could establish undoubtedly that in no case were his signatures identical. He demanded a new expertise, and they discovered that the signatures on both incriminating letters were perfectly identical and on this basis, the experts acknowledged that the signatures were forged, and subsequently it was found that the letters were written by enemies of K. to ruin him. He was acquitted and released on the fortieth day after his arrest. This was exactly the period that his sister had mentioned in his first dream when she pushed him into a black pit.

Some facts are known about the human mind and memory which cannot be explained by science. Under certain conditions things long forgotten may be remembered. It has since long been known that in the mind of the dying man just before death his whole life may unfold with a remarkable clarity and an incredible speed. Fechner tells us about a woman who had fallen into the water and nearly drowned. Two minutes passed after all movements of her body had stopped till she was taken out of the water, during which time she, in her words said she once again lived through all her past life unfolding before her innner eyes in the smallest details.

Admiral Boffre gives another example of such a stream of images in which the memories of many years pass in a short time through the human mind. He fell into the water and lost consciousness. He says, "In this state, one thought was followed by another so fast that it was neither possible to describe nor conceivable for anyone having not experienced this." First, he imagined the direct consequences of his death to his family, but then his spiritual eyes turned to the past: once again he lived through his voyage and shipwreck, his school days, his years of study and the time he had wasted; even all his childhood, his journeys and mischief. He says: "While going further into the past, in my memory I saw facts in my life in a reverse order of their natural sequence, and not in vague outlines, but in a very clear picture in the smallest details. In short, my whole life passed before my soul as a panorama, and each step was accompanied by the awareness of its right or wrong, the precise understanding of its causes and effects. Many minor adventures of my life, in fact, already forgotten, appeared before my spiritual eyes with the same clarity as if they had happened recently."

In this case, at the most two minutes passed from Boffre's falling into water till getting him out.

If in these cases T. Ribot tries to explain the uncanny speed of the flow of consciousness by the state of asphyxia (suffocation), this explanation however is totally not applicable to the following case reported by him.

A man who had an amazingly bright mind, was stepping over train rails at the moment that a train was suddenly approaching at full speed. He had no choice but to lie down between the rails. And while vans were passing over this man, who was almost paralysed from fear, the sense of danger made him remember all the events of his life as if the pages of the Doomsday book were unfolding before his eyes. In the same way, when people die, the "film" of their life from beginning to end, unfolds itself within an instance in their consciousness.

Sekkendorf saw in his dream those events of his past life, which he barely remembered, and with such clarity and vividness, as if they just happened. With extraordinary clarity he saw himself as a three-year-old child and all the smallest details of his upbringing were revived in his memory. Each mark at school, every unpleasant incident were perceived in his consciousness as if just happening. Contemplating his life in the right sequence of events, he saw finally, his stay in Italy, where he had left a lady, whom he would have married if fate had not forced him to leave the country quickly. That sharp feeling of separation from his beloved lively experienced by him in the dream was the cause of his awakening.

If such a sudden remembrance of life is possible for the dying, and even in a dream, it becomes clear how "The Doomsday Book" will be revealed to our consciousness at the Last Judgment.

In the book "Studies of Animal Magnetism" we find a report of John Everdtveger, who after a long illness fell into a deathlike state which lasted for several hours. When he opened his eyes he told his confessor that he had seen all his life, all his sins, even those that had long been erased from his memory. The vision was so vivid, as if he experienced it for the first time. The ability of such a phantasmagorical re-experiencing of their entire life by the dying, accompanied by the compression of years of their life into just a few seconds, and the contemplation of individual phases of their life as degrees of development of their spiritual being, was already known in ancient times and was considered a distinctive ability of the human soul. The philosopher Plotinus says in "Enneads": "But over time, by the end of life memories of the earlier periods of existence appear... because, released from the body, it (our soul) recollects that what it didn't remember here." In these amazing facts of the two - three minutes lasting reproduction of the events of a lifetime, which lasted decades, we are struck first by the preternatural speed of recollection, and secondly by the amazing completeness and clarity of them.

Let us discuss the first point. Images of memories rush in our consciousness with a transcendental rapidity when smoking opium or hashish. T. Ribot in his book "Diseases of the Memory" writes the confession of Kepsey, a passionate opium smoker. He says that while intoxicated he had dreams, lasting ten, twenty, thirty, sixty years; even those that surpass apparently, all thinkable limitations of human life. Insignificant events of his youth, forgotten scenes of the early years of his life often rose before him. He could not say that he remembered them, because if he had been told about them when awake, he would not have recognized his past life in them. But when they passed before him like a dream, in a long-forgotten atmosphere and feelings, then he immediately recognized them.

How can we explain this uncanny quickness of the recollections? In physiology it is known that all processes in the nervous system require a certain time, although very small, measuring fractions of a second. The longer the nerve the greater is the time required for the passage of stimuli from the receptor through the sensitive nerve. Some time is required for the formation of a response in nerve cells, which received this stimulation; some time is required for the transfer of the reaction along the motor nerve. All mental and sensory processes that take place in the brain need time. And if it were possible to summarise and calculate the time of all the mental processes that occur throughout our lives, it would have been a very considerable amount of time. Consequently, it is impossible that this recollection of an entire life which takes just a moment can occur inside the material brain.

Therefore we may conclude that it does not occur inside the brain.

Where else then? As we have said, the life of the spirit is inseparably and intimately connected with all the neuro-psychic activity. It is there, in the spirit that all our thoughts, feelings, volitions, i.e. everything that occurs in our phenomenal consciousness, is imprinted. And this is something different to those tracks and impresses in the nerve cells, which physiologists and psychologists consider to be the mechanism of memory.

We, of course, are far from denying the existence and necessity of such traces and impresses in nerve cells and their rightful explanation of many, perhaps even all the usual functions of the memory. The gradual decline and even disappearance of the memory caused by senile dementia, of course, depends on the atrophy and dying of nerve cells of the cerebral cortex which may be reduced to half or even to one-third of their number. We also know that memory can fade through damage to the brain medulla or cortex after a trauma or an infection. Therefore, the explanation of memory in its most complicated forms by the theory of molecular traces in the brain cells and associative fibres does not satisfy us at all. Although the nerve cells do not proliferate and are not replaced by new ones, like all other organs and tissues, but only die, yet there are continuous exchanges in them, and very likely changes in their molecules. How could we imagine any adequate mechanism for fixing and maintaining forever the traces of all mental acts? And how possibly do we have the right to talk about saving these tracks forever if we know how fragile the memory is and how much of it disappears irretrievably?

The other aspect is even more important. It is impossible to consider the anatomical substrate of memory to be the impresses in just one cell, for in the memory there should be imprinted the impresses of mental acts, which are always complex and involve the participation of the set of cells and association fibres. In the brain there must be kept the impresses not of individual changes in single cells, but the chains of "dynamic associations", according to T. Ribot. During a lifetime quite an incalculable number of such dynamic associations, which constantly change each other, occur in the brain. Their number is as immense as the number of metres from the earth to Sirius. A number of brain cells however, though very large (6 billion according to Meinert), are still quite insignificant compared to the number of mental processes which are supposed to be impressed in them. That is why only some impressions, the most vivid ones are stored in the memory, and it is impossible that the brain could preserve forever the impresses of all the smallest events of our lives with all their details, their sensuous tinge and moral evaluation.

Therefore, we must recognize that, beside the brain there must be another, much more significant and powerful substrate of memory. And we believe such a substrate to be the human spirit, where all our psycho-physical acts are impressed forever. For the manifestation of the spirit there is no time limit, it does not need any sequence or relation of cause and effect for the recollection of the experiences in the memory as are necessary for the brain function.

The spirit embraces all at once and instantly reproduces it in its integrity.

In addition, we believe it is appropriate to remember Richet's valuable words: "The Spirit can operate without consciousness knowing about it: the very complex mental activities pass through our consciousness unnoticeably. A whole world of ideas unknown to us, trembles within us." Probably no recollection of the past is blotted out. Consciousness forgets much, memory forgets nothing. The whole set of images of the past remains almost unchanged, although they have disappeared from our consciousness. For the unconscious stays awake. If we assume that all the richness of memory is kept in full power in the spirit, the amazing phenomena of hypermnesia reported by many authors becomes clear. Let's just mention a few examples. Many authors have reported the amazing facts of long forgotten languages being memorized. A man, who had left his homeland Wales, in childhood and had quite forgotten the Welsh language, in a fit of delirium seventy years later spoke Welsh fluently, but on recovery could not say a word in that language.

Farihagen observed a basket-weaver who had heard a sermon on repentance that had deeply touched him. The next night, he got out of bed still sleeping, and repeated that entire sermon with literal accuracy, pacing up and down his bedroom. When he woke up he couldn't repeat it. And even forty years later he often recited excerpts from that sermon when talking to someone.

A farmer from Rostov, Russia, being in a feverish delirium, suddenly began to say the opening words of the Gospel of John in Greek which he had accidently heard 60 years ago. Seneca mentioned a peasant woman, who being in a feverish delirium pronounced Syrian, Chaldean and Hebrew words which she heard accidentally from a scientist with whom she lived in her childhood. Even the observations made on idiots have shown not only hypermnesia, but also an amazing display of a hidden conscious life.

Maudsley in his book "Physiology and Pathology of the Soul" says: "The extraordinary memory of some idiots who, despite the limitations of their minds reproduce the longest narrations with great accuracy, provides further evidence in favour of such unconscious activity of the soul. Many idiots in a state of excitement caused, for example by great grief or other reasons (for example, the lastupsurge of fading life)show they are capable of such an inner life for which they were apparently, made forever incapable, and this indicates that many things that they can't express are perceived by them and leave impresses in their souls."

There are not enough words to express just how true it is that our consciousness does not comprise our soul. Consciousness can't give us a report on the way these impresses are formed and how exactly they are kept in our soul in a latent state.

T. Ribot tries to explain hypermnesia by an increased blood flow in the brain caused by fever. But this explanation is clearly untenable, since hypermnesia has been observed during sleep also, when the activity of the cerebral cortex is strongly suppressed. If hypermnesia occurs in two opposite states of the brain, sleep and excitement during delirious fever, they can't be its cause, but only a [suitable] occasion for it to be manifested. This is what we"ll discuss in detail in the next chapter. The correctness of our explanation of memory is shown and approved in the Scriptures. The Medium of Endor called the spirit of the Prophet Samuel on request of king Saul, and the conversation of king Saul with the ghost of the Prophet Samuel (1 Sam. 28: 13 - 15) suggests that Samuel's spirit preserved also after his death all the memories of his military life, all the abilities of the mind, will and feelings. It's definitely the same for Moses and Elijah who appeared at the Lord's Transfiguration on Mount Tabor.

How could the dead appear before their loved ones and talk to them if their spirit had not retained all the memories of their life on earth? The little brother could see and hear his dead brother, who called on him to follow him. The little girl saw and heard her dead aunt Louise, who appeared to her many times and called her to join her in the world behind the curtain. His dead father foretold Metropolitan Philaret his death on the 19th day. This list can easily be continued.

Chapter 8. On the inner Man

From all these facts, new and old, we conclude once again: there are in nature unknown "vibrations' which set the human intellect into motion and reveal to it facts inaccessible to man's five senses.
If we acknowledge the existence of telepathy, we must change only one word in this assumption. It is enough to say "vibrations" of human thought, instead of talking about the "unknown vibration". However, reducing cryptaesthesia to just "vibration of human thought" means an extreme confining of the concept of cryptaesthesia and, consequently, perverting it.
We have talked about it many times with people "devoid of superstition", who "believe in science only", and they always found a simple explanation for all these "new and terrible things". These are just "the waves of human thought", the "oscillations of the molecules of the human brain", which spread like waves transmitted through the wireless. Blessed are the people for whom everything is so simple and clear. They need not weary their superficial thinking with the hard work of studying and clarifying the new and the unknown. They always explain new and extraordinary facts by old and ordinary ones. Science is the only authority for them, although its axioms and hypotheses often crumble like a house of cards under the pressure of the new and unknown. They simply dismiss as superstition and old wives' tales everything that does not fit in the old scientific framework. They can accept a new vision only by getting used to it. Well, even horses stopped being frightened by cars when they got used to them. If physics recognizes the wave-like motion as the basis of material phenomena, why must it necessarily be applicable to

the phenomena of a higher order which occur in the immaterial world?

Why not admit that other laws are valid in that [immaterial] world, which are very different and unknown to us, and that the spiritual energy, the energy of love, sympathy and antipathy, may act beyond time and space, without requiring a wave-like motion?

Let us put a simple question to the "devoid of superstition": if all metaphysic phenomena, all forms of cryptaesthesia are explained by the movement of brain particles transmitted by waves through space, how should we apply this explanation to the undoubted facts of communicating with the dead , whose brain no longer exists?

The profound scientist C. Richet poses far more difficult questions. "From all these facts, both the important and the less important ones, we should make the conclusion which the petty critics cannot make. This conclusion is that the foreboding, predictions are proven facts: strange, paradoxical, absurd facts judging by their appearance, but facts that we have to recognize. So, under some not yet exactly defined conditions, certain individuals, most often (though not exclusively) easily hypnotized people, or mediums, can predict events and report on facts that have not yet happened and which can't be foreseen, in such precise detail, that these predictions cannot be explained by perspicacity, coincidence, or occasion.

We have to assume that having a special mystical knowledge, the nature and characteristics of which are not known to us, which we call cryptaesthesia may be found not only in relation to the past and the present, but also in relation to the future. In addition, the metaphysic knowledge of the present is so unusual that our knowledge of the future is even a little more amazing. A. knows that B. who is a thousand miles away has just drowned. How could A. possibly know? We have no answers. A. predicts that B. will drown tomorrow. This is a little bit more mysterious, but not much more. In the field of metaphysic clairvoyance the oddity is so overwhelming, and the obscurity is so enigmatic that a little more obscurity and oddity should not confuse us.

I will not enter into useless speculations. I will keep to the dense area of facts. So, there are proven facts, indisputable facts of foresight. The explanation will come later (or will not come). However, there are facts, credible, irrefutable facts. Anticipation and foresight exist. Is it only due to the power of human intellect, or are there some other intellectual forces which affect our intellect? It is impossible to find out presently. Let us be satisfied with at least communicating the facts precisely as they are. It would be an unforgivable audacity for us to claim that there is a prediction if there had not been ample evidence of it." (Richet)

What do the words in the Song of Solomon mean: "I sleep but my heart awaketh?" (Song 5: 2). These are very profound words. The heart is the organ of higher cognition, the organ of communication with God and with the entire transcendental world, and it never sleeps. The most important and profound mental activity takes place beyond the threshold of our consciousness, and it never stops. A clear expression of this idea can be found in Leibniz' works.

"Our own experience shows that there is no moment of life, when there would be a pause in the designing power, and the spirit would cease forming designs. Wouldn't opponents talk about the dream world? But sleep has its images ; in fact, it is full of dreams, and we dream constantly. The so-called sleep without dreams is nothing but the deep sleep, with dreams we don't remember and have no idea of their images when waking up. But upon awakening we always have a feeling that during sleep a certain time has passed, and this feeling would be impossible if we had not dreamed, i.e. if there had not been images during our sleep, because we always measure time by the images which took place so the same time seems longer or shorter depending on the number of images we had.

If we didn't dream at all, we would perceive the time of our sleep as non-existant; however as the passed dream seems to us a certain passed time, this experience sufficiently proves that we constantly have images. In addition, we would not wake up having ideas in our mind if we slept without any images. However, the so-called sleep without dreams is accompanied by a weak sensation of the outside world, and the stronger this feeling is, the more easily we wake up. That is why continuity of the images in our soul should not be based on our dreams only, for the dream contains also images of the outside world."

Almost all people, even the least sensitive, have the ability of higher knowledge, different from the knowledge of the five senses. The more spiritual a man is, the more pronounced is his ability for higher cognition. Under special circumstances and in highly sensitive people it is manifested by an extraordinary power of clairvoyance, premonition and prophetic anticipation as the unknown and mysterious sixth sense, through which they learn a lot about people by their belongings. We mentioned many facts of such supernatural cognition. In most of these cases the organism and first of all the brain of these people was in an abnormal state. This was the state of hypnosis, somnambulism, febrile delirium, or of a medium. But it was not always so.

In a smaller number of cases such supernatural abilities are manifested by people who are in a normal state. Speaking of the facts of transcendental abilities and somnambulism in a state of hypnosis, we have more than once compared them with similar facts from the lives of saints, or even of ordinary people.

What does this mean? This means that for the manifestation of the transcendental powers of our spirit, for the detection of super-consciousness it is necessary to "switch off", or at least significantly weaken our normal phenomenal consciousness. To express this idea Du Prel makes a good comparison: stars give light constantly, but we do not see their light when the sun is shining. It is necessary for the sun to set and the darkness of night to come, and then the light of the stars becomes visible for us.

As long as our life proceeds in the kaleidoscope and the noise of external perceptions while our phenomenal consciousness is running at full power, the never-ending activity of the super-consciousness is concealed from us. But during the normal sleep, the somnambulistic or hypnotic one, or when the brain is poisoned with opium, or hashish, or toxins of febrile illnesses, our normal brain activity and the light of phenomenal consciousness are quenched, and then the light of transcendental consciousness flares up. We also know that blindness deepens the work of thought and moral sense and widens the threshold of consciousness. The philosopher Fechner created his most profound works after having become blind. Prince Basil the Dark said to Shemyaka, the man who had blinded him: "You gave me the means to repent." It is known from the lives of many saints that long, debilitating illnesses were a great blessing for them, for they tamed their passions, deprived them of the impressions of life in the world with its noise and bustle, which distract from going deeper into the recesses of the spirit. This is well understood and deeply appreciated by the Christian and Buddhist anchorites who sought the suppression of all external impressions through a life in seclusion, the constant immersion in oneself and prayer; to subdue the flesh to the spirit by fasting and vigil, even by standing on a pillar.

In the martyrology there are many examples of the heaviest injuries to the body, the most cruel tortures causing the extinction of the phenomenal consciousness and the awakening of the inner transcendental consciousness which manifests itself by inner bliss.

Transcendental life of the spirit was well known to the ancient Indian sages and Greek philosophers, especially philosophers of the Alexandrian school. Plotinus, Porphyry, and others wrote about it. Here are the words of Plotinus: "Finally, if I dare to express freely and definitely my own belief in opposition to the opinion of other people, then, I think that in the sensual body there constantly remains not all of our soul, but only a part of it, which, being immersed in this world and therefore condensing, or rather, becoming clogged and darkened, prevents us to percept the same what the highest part of our soul perceives." In another place he says: "The souls are like amphibians: they live, according to their need, sometimes on this side of the living, and sometimes in the afterlife." Paracelsus, Van Helmont, Campanella, and many others expressed similar ideas during the Renaissance.

In "German Theology", composed by Luther and highly valued by Schopenhauer, it is said: "The created human soul has two eyes: one can contemplate the eternal, the other only temporary and created things. But these two eyes of our soul can't do their job both at once, but only so that when our soul is contemplating the eternity with its right eye, its left eye should entirely abandon all its activities and remain in idleness, like being dead. When the left eye is operating, and the soul has to deal with the temporal and made, then its right eye should give up all activity. So, who wants to watch with one eye only should get rid of the other, for no man can serve two masters".

Emmanuel Kant undoubtedly recognized the transcendental subject in an unattainable depth of his thought. His contemporaries had little interest in the magical powers of the human soul, and had a poor faith in them. But Kant, with his powerful logic, never judged anything with preconceived ideas and considered impossible only the ideas containing logical contradictions. He argued that we can prescribe nothing to the experience and should take from it all that it gives us, even if it may seem strange and unexpected to us. So when he learned about the discovery of the magical powers of Swedenborg, his contemporary, Kant not only collected accurate information about that mystic, but also bought his works. After reading them, he was struck by the similarity of Swedenborg's theory with his own, drawn from pure reason, the theory of the transcendental nature of man.

In "The Dreams of a Spirit-Seer" Kant writes: "I confess that I am very inclined to believing in the existence of immaterial beings in the world, and to reckon my own soul as such a creature." And then he adds: "Therefore, the human soul in this life should be considered simultaneously connected with both worlds, but while still being united with the body, it perceives clearly only the material world."

In "Rosencrantz" Kant expresses his thought even more clearly: "Therefore we can assume almost for granted, or easily proved, ... or, rather, it will be proved, although I do not know where or when, that the human soul in this life is in close connection with all immaterial beings of the spiritual world, that it operates alternately in the one or the other world, and perceives from those beings impressions, which it, being an earthly man, is not aware of until everything goes well (that is, until it enjoys the material world)."

Kant always kept to his teaching about "things in themselves", which he reckoned to the world of noumenons. Kant's "noumenon man" is what he called "a thing in itself", and Carl Du Prel called it a "transcendental I", and the Apostle Paul called it "the inner man." For us of course, the most important are the words of the Apostle Paul: "Though our outward man perish, yet the inward man is renewed day by day." (2 Cor. 4:16) When out of passion and lust the flesh weakens and fades, when its strength is weakened, and the glamour and noise of this world cloud us, then " ...put off concerning the former conversation the old man, which is corrupt according to the deceitful lusts, and renewed in the spirit of our mind, and that ye put on the new man, which after God is created in righteousness and true holiness." (Eph. 4: 22 - 24)

"The New Man" in the words of Paul, is of course the same as the "inner man".

This deep psychological change occurs in us through the action of God's Grace: "By reason of this grace, I bend my knees to the Father of our Lord Jesus Christ, from whom all paternity in heaven and on earth takes its name.

And I ask him to grant to you to be strengthened in virtue by his Spirit, in accord with the wealth of his glory, in the inner man." (Eph. 3:14-16)

Then there is a co-crucifixion with Christ of our old "outer" man to destroy the body full of sin, for "we may no longer serve sin." (Rom. 6:6), and then "Instead, you should be a hidden person of the heart, with the incorruptibility of a quiet and meek spirit, rich in the sight of God." (1 Pet. 3:4)

Then we even become "partakers of the Divine nature" according to the words of the Apostle Peter (2 Pet. 1:4), then "Christ may live in your hearts through a faith rooted in, and founded on, charity.

So may you be able to embrace, with all the saints, what is the width and length and height and depth of the charity of Christ, and even be able to know that which surpasses all knowledge, so that you may be filled with all the fullness of God." (Eph. 3:17-19)

And we should add another words of Paul: ".Strip yourselves of the old man, with his deeds, and clothe yourself with the new man, who has been renewed by knowledge, in accord with the image of the One who created him." (Col. 3: 9 -10)

Our inner, transcendental man, freed from the bonds of the flesh, can reach the highest knowledge of all that exists in all its "breadth and length, and depth and height", for he will be renewed and strengthened in the knowledge, even according to his creation in the image of his Creator, he will comprehend the love of Christ surpassing all earthly understanding, for Christ will dwell in him by faith. Incomprehensible to the "geometrical mind" it becomes clear to the transcendental consciousness of the inner man enlightened by Christ.

Chapter 9. Immortality

The human spirit is the breath of the Spirit of God, and for this reason only it is immortal, like all incorporeal, angelic spirits. They are numerous, as evidenced by the Scriptures, and the extent of their development, their perfection is infinite.

In the range of earthly beings man is the first and the only spiritual being, and there have been people of a very high degree of spirituality, almost liberating the spirit from the body during their life. These human-angels ascended into the air during their prayer, manifested the greatest power of the spirit over the body (the pillar ascetics, fasters); they were in a transitional stage between the spirit associated with the body and the soul (a person) and the bodiless spirit (an angel).

The whole world of living beings, even the whole of nature, demonstrates the great law of the endless gradual improvement of forms, and it is impossible to assume that the utter perfection achieved in the earth's nature, the spirituality of man, had no further development beyond the physical world. It is impossible to assume that all the innumerable worlds of stars were just vast masses of dead matter, and that the world of living beings ended with man, who is just the first stage of spiritual development. What prevents us from assuming that the heavenly bodies are the dwellings of countless sentient living beings, who possess higher forms of intelligence?

There are the usual arguments against it, namely that organic life is impossible under the physical conditions existing on the stars and the planets (except perhaps, Mars). But do the bodiless spirits need certain physical conditions of life, like organic beings? And finally, why couldn't forms of physicality exist there, very different from the ones on earth, adapted to physical conditions different from ours?

And the glowing white-hot surface of huge stars may be inhabited by fiery seraphim and cherubim: "You make your Angels a breath of life, and your ministers a burning fire." (Ps. 103(104):4)

If the law of development and improvement in the earth's nature is so clear, there is no reason to suppose that it is suspended outside our planet, that the spirit first manifested in man, but being evident even in the simplest creatures in the initial form, has no further development in the Universe.

The world has its origin in God's Love, and if people are given the law: "Therefore, be perfect, even as your heavenly Father is perfect." (Matthew 5:48), then, of course, they must be given the opportunity for this commandment to be implemented, that is the possibility of infinite perfection of the spirit. And this requires the everlasting existence of the immortal spirit and the infinite number of forms of its perfection. It couldn't be so, that the law of the infinite perfection of the spirit in its approach to the perfection of God was given to people only, not to the whole universe, not to the whole world of spiritual beings, for they are created in various degrees of perfection, far exceeding the smallest perfection of the human spirit.

If matter and energy in their physical form are perfect (indestructible), then, of course, the spiritual energy, or, in other words, the spirit of man and all living beings, should be subjected to this law. Thus, immortality is a necessary postulate of our mind.

Our Lord Jesus Christ openly testified the immortality of man: "And everyone who lives and believes in me shall not die for eternity." (John 11:26)

"whoever hears my word, and believes in him who sent me, has eternal life." (John 5: 24)

And the Apostle James speaks of a man as of just the first stage of spirituality; he particularly says: "For by his own will he produced us through the Word of truth, so that we might be a kind of beginning among his creatures." (James 1:18) And Paul says: "and not only these, but also ourselves, since we hold the first-fruits of the Spirit." (Rom. 8:23) There is no need of any other proof of immortality for us, Christians. And for the disbelievers it is useful to recall the words of Emmanuel Kant, the most profound of people, cited in the previous chapter. He believed in the existence of incorporeal and therefore immortal beings in the world, and his own soul he reckoned as one of them. C. Richet at the end of his great book, where a huge amount of undoubted metaphysic facts were gathered, discusses possible explanations, and concludes that the most probable of them should be seen in the existence of beings possessing reason other than the humans that surround us, and who can interfere in our life, in our development, although they are alien to the mechanical, physical, anatomical and chemical conditions of existence.

Why should we not acknowledge the existence of intelligent, powerful beings not belonging to the world of our senses? By what right do we, with our limited senses, our imperfect minds, our scientific development, which is just three centuries old, dare to say that man is the only being in the immeasurable space to possess reason, and that any thinking reality depends on the presence of nerve cells, irrigated with blood? The existence of intelligent beings different from humans, having an entirely different type of organization to the human, is not only possible but highly probable. It is absurd to think that the human mind is unique in the universe, and that any power which possesses reason must necessarily be organized the same way as man or animals, and have a brain as the organ of thought.

If we assume that in the universe, in the time and the space that our rudimentary psychology is subjected to, there are powers endowed with reason which sometimes interfere in our lives, we obtain a hypothesis which gives a full explanation of the facts stated in this book.

Thus acknowledging the existence of non-material forms of mystical creatures, angels or demons, spirits, who sometimes interfere in our actions, creatures who may change our matter by their will through ways completely unknown to us, direct some of our thoughts, take part in our lives; creatures who can take the bodily and psychological form of the dead to enter into communication with us (the only way for us to know them) is the easiest way to understand and explain much of the metaphysic phenomena.

This is the conclusion of a scientist used to positive thinking, obtained after the objective study of many metaphysic facts, which he assiduously collected during his lifetime.

Other prominent scientists in the fields of metapsychology, Mauer and Oliver Lodge, arrived at a similar conclusion.

The essence of this conclusion may be reduced to the statement that the human spirit communicating with the transcendental, eternal world, lives in it and belongs to eternity.

The main obstacle to unbelievers admitting the soul's immortality is the dualistic conception of body and soul, the idea of the soul as a distinct entity, just associated with the body during its lifetime.

This view is exactly what we consider being the core of disbelief and in the Scriptures we find no obstacle to understanding the relation between soul and body from the point of view of monism. We have already spoken about the necessary connection between the spirit and the form, about the fact that the spirit forms the body in the embryonic stage of its growth. Spiritual energy is inherent in all the cells of the body as they are alive and the life comes from the Spirit.

There is, of course, the two-way causal relationship between all the functions of the body and psychic activity, interpreted by psychologists.

But this concerns only that part of our threefold being, which could be called the lower, animal soul; it is that part of our spiritual essence which is embraced by our consciousness: it is, so to speak, our "phenomenal" soul. And "The Spirit projects outside the brain from all sides" (Bergson); the spirit is the sum of our soul and its part lying outside the boundaries of our consciousness.

There is constant communication and interaction between the body and the spirit. Everything that happens in the soul of a man throughout his life has its meaning and is necessary only because the whole life of our soul and body, every thought, feeling, volition, having started in sensory perceptions, is closely connected with the life of the spirit. All acts of the body and the soul are imprinted in the spirit, and are kept in it, and form it. The life of the spirit and its orientation towards good or evil evolves under their formative influence. The life of the brain and the heart, and the entire, marvellously coordinated life of all organs of the body are necessary only for the formation of the spirit and they cease when its formation is completed, or its direction has become definite. The life of the body and the soul can be compared with the life of a bunch of grapes full of beauty and charm. The moment comes when it is no longer fed with the juice of the vine and the dew from heaven sprinkled on the gentle bloom of the grapes ceases, and they become just pressed skins, doomed to decay; but the life of grapes goes on in the wine obtained from them. All that was valuable, beautiful and fragrant, that has been produced in living grapes under the beneficial influence of light and heat from the sun, goes into the wine. And just as wine does not spoil, but continues to live its own life after the death of the grapes, becoming better and more valuable the longer it lives, so the eternal life goes on in the immortal human spirit as well as an infinite development in the way of good or evil after the death of the body, brain and heart, when the soul is not longer active.

We understand the eternal bliss of the righteous and the eternal torment of sinners to mean that the immortal spirit of the righteous, enlightened and powerfully amplified after the liberation from the body, has the possibility of an infinite development towards God's goodness and love, in constant communication with God and all His bodiless powers. While the dark spirit of the wicked and those opposing God, which is in constant communication with the devil and his angels, will be eternally tormented because it is alienated from God, Whose sanctity will finally become evident to it, and because of the unbearable poison full of evil and hate, which infinitely augment through the constant communication with the centre and source of evil, Satan.

It is certainly impossible to blame God for the eternal torment of sinners, thinking of Him as infinitely vindictive, punishing with eternal torment the sins of a short-lived life. Each person receives and possesses the breath of the Holy Spirit. No one is born of the spirit of Satan. But as the dark clouds obscure the sun and absorb light, so the evil acts of the mind, of the will and of the feelings by their constant repetition and prevalence darken constantly the light of Christ in the soul of an evil man, and his mind becomes more and more determined by the influence of the spirit of the devil. They who loved evil rather than good, have prepared for themselves eternal torment in the life everlasting.

But here we are confronted with an ancient dispute on free will and determinism.

Only the great Kant gave a profound solution to this dispute. Freedom can't be attributed to man as a phenomenon of the material world, because he is subjected to causality in this world. Like everything in nature, he has his own empirical character, which determines his reactions to external stimuli.

But in his spirit man belongs to the noumenal, transcendental world, thus his reaction to external stimuli is determined not only by his empirical character, but also by his spirit. Kant says, "Thus, freedom and necessity each in its full meaning can co-exist and do not contradict each other in the same act, as our every act is the product of noumenal and sensible reasons."

Simply put, the human spirit is free, "blows where it wishes..." And its lower, perceptible soul obeys the laws of causality.

We have still spoken only of the immortality of the spirit, but also our bodies will be resurrected to eternal life and they will be partaking in the endless blissfulness of the righteous or the interminable torment of sinners according to the clear testimony of Revelation.

This is also a stumbling block to unbelievers and a great mystery for the faithful. The unbelievers find impossible the restoration and resurrection of the bodies, which were completely destroyed by decay or burnt, turned to dust and gases, decomposed to atoms. But if during the life of the body the spirit was intimately connected with it, with all its organs and tissues, penetrating all the molecules and atoms of the body, if it was its organizing source, why should the relationship disappear forever after the death of the body? Why is it unthinkable that this relationship is preserved for ever after death, and at the universal resurrection at the sound of the archangel's trumpet the immortal spirit will be reconnected with all the physical and chemical elements of the rotted body, and the organizing power of the spirit, creating forms, will manifest itself again? Nothing disappears, it is just modified.

Another difficult issue, which is a mystery to believers, is understanding the purpose of the resurrection of the dead in their earthly integrity. The immortality of the spirit freed from the bondage of the body is clearer for us. Why is it necessary for the whole man to participate in eternal life, not only the spirit, but also his body and soul?

Of course, we can't clearly comprehend the mystery of God ruling over His creation, yet the Scriptures give us the opportunity to lift the veil. The Holy Apostles Peter and John to some extent explain the secrets of the resurrection of human bodies. They speak clearly about the end of the world, the great and terrible catastrophe which will occur in the universe at the time of the second coming of the Lord Jesus Christ.

"Then the day of the Lord shall arrive like a thief. On that day, the heavens shall pass away with great violence, and truly the elements shall be dissolved with heat; then the earth, and the works that are within it, shall be completely burned up." (2 Pet. 3:10)

And the Apostle John in his Revelation clearly depicts this world catastrophe divided into phases.

What will be next? What is the purpose of this cataclysm?

"Yet truly, in accord with his promises, we are looking forward to the new heavens and the new earth, in which justice lives." (2 Pet. 3:13)

"I saw the new heaven and the new earth. For the first heaven and the first earth passed away, and the sea is no more.

And I, John, saw the Holy City, the New Jerusalem, descending out of heaven from God, prepared like a bride adorned for her husband.

And I heard a great voice from the throne, saying: "Behold the tabernacle of God with men. And he will dwell with them, and they will be his people. And God himself will be their God with them.

And God will wipe away every tear from their eyes. And death shall be no more. And neither mourning, nor crying out, nor grief shall be anymore. For the first things have passed away."

And the One who was sitting upon the throne, said, "Behold, I make all things new."" (Rev. 21:1-5)

"I make all things new". There will be a time for the new creation, the new earth and the new heavens. Everything will be completely different, and our new life will take place in a totally new environment, and we should have our full nature in that life and perceive a quite new experience by our renewed and enlightened senses. Consequently, the activity of the part of our spirit, that we now call the lower, physiological soul, will be necessary.

Our thoughts will work hard to discover the new world, where our spirit, freed from the power of the earth, from our sinful flesh, will be built and strive to come closer to God. The mind is a part of our spirit, and therefore our brains have to be immortal, too. The immortal heart will be the focus of new, pure and deep feelings.

The eternal life is not only the life of the spirit, freed from the body and soul, but the life in the New Jerusalem, described so vividly by St. John the Theologian in his "Revelation".

The immortality of the body, not just the spirit, perhaps has one more purpose, full of justice and truth, i.e. the purpose of honouring the body of the saints as the great instrument of the spirit, which worked hard and suffered during the formation and perfection of the spirit during the earthly life. And the bodies of grave sinners, which were the principal instruments of sin, of course deserve punishment. The powerful and terrible pictures of Dante's "Inferno" are probably not just a figment of poetic imagination.

St. Paul reveals to a significant extent the mystery of the resurrection of the bodies in his first epistle to the Corinthians: ""How do the dead rise again?" or, "What type of body do they return with?"

How foolish! What you sow cannot be brought back to life, unless it first dies.

And what you sow is not the body that will be in the future, but a bare grain, such as of wheat, or of some other grain.
For God gives it a body according to his will, and according to each seed's proper body.
Not all flesh is the same flesh. But one is indeed of men, another truly is of beasts, another is of birds, and another is of fish.
Also, there are heavenly bodies and earthly bodies. But while the one, certainly, has the glory of heaven, the other has the glory of earth.
One has the brightness of the sun, another the brightness of the moon, and another the brightness of the stars. For even star differs from star in brightness.
So it is also with the resurrection of the dead. What is sown in corruption shall rise to incorruption.
What is sown in dishonor shall rise to glory. What is sown in weakness shall rise to power.
What is sown with an animal body shall rise with a spiritual body. If there is an animal body, there is also a spiritual one." (1Cor.15: 35-44)
Sown, buried in the ground, the grain as if perishes; it ceases to exist as a seed, but out of it there grows something much larger than it was, incomparably better in its complexity and form, a new plant. God gives it shape and beauty, and life full of utility and delights.@@@@@
A human body is buried in the ground, and it ceases to exist as a body. But from the elements in which it is decomposed, as from cells of grains of wheat, the power of God will raise a new body, and not a destroyed, weak and powerless corpse, but a new spiritual body, full of power, incorruption and glory.
"The first man is of the earth, earthy: the second man is the Lord from heaven. As is the earthy, such are they also that are earthy: and as is the heavenly, such are they also that are

heavenly. And as we have borne the image of the earthy, we shall also bear the image of the heavenly." (1 Cor. 15:47-49)
During life our body is of dust, of soul, as the body of Adam. After the resurrection it will be different, spiritual, like the heavenly body of the second Adam, Jesus Christ, the one he had after His glorious Resurrection.
We do not know all the properties of the resurrected body of Jesus Christ. We only know that it passed through locked doors, could suddenly disappear from sight. (Luke 24:36; John 20: 19).
He was not immediately recognized by the apostles and the myrrh-bearing women. The Lord ascended into heaven in this glorious body. But it was a real body, which the apostles could touch, and it could have the usual functions of the human body (Luke 24:43). Our body will be similar to the body of Christ after our resurrection to eternal life.
Does only man possess immortality? The great words: "Behold, I make all things new" are certainly related not to man only, but to all creation, to every creature. We have already said that the spirit of animals, even the smallest part of it, the spirit of life, cannot be mortal, for it is from the Holy Spirit. And the spirit of animals is connected with the body, like the spirit of man, and therefore there is all reason to expect that their bodies will exist in the new nature also, in the new universe which comes after the end of this world. This is evidenced by the Apostle Paul: "For the anticipation of the creature anticipates the revelation of the sons of God.
For the creature was made subject to emptiness, not willingly, but for the sake of the One who made it subject, unto hope. For the creature itself shall also be delivered from the servitude of corruption, into the liberty of the glory of the sons of God.
For we know that every creature groans inwardly, as if giving birth, even until now; and not only these, but also ourselves,

since we hold the first-fruits of the Spirit. For we also groan within ourselves, anticipating our adoption as the sons of God, and the redemption of our body." (Rom. 8:19-23)

All the creatures would have lived in light and joy, if the sinful Adam's fall had not changed the destinies of the world. The fate of the world became sad, and according to the sinful will of Adam, to whom God had subjected it, it has become subjected to vanity, discord and suffering. But there is hope for it, that on the day of glorifying all the righteous, redeemed by Christ from the bondage of corruption, it will be freed from suffering and decay, i.e. will become imperishable.

In the new Jerusalem, the new universe, there will be a place for the animals, too; there will be nothing unclean there, and the new creature will regain the old justification and sanctification by God's Word: "And God saw everything that he had made. And they were very good." (Gen. 1:31)

Certainly, immortality will not be of the same value for animals as for man. Its primitive spirit can't grow infinitely and be morally improved. Eternal life for the low creatures will be only quiet happiness and enjoyment of the new radiant nature full of light, in communication with man, who will no longer torture and exterminate it. Man will be whole and harmonious in the future new universe, and there will be a place for every creature in it.

God bless! God bless!

www.ingramcontent.com/pod-product-compliance
Lightning Source LLC
LaVergne TN
LVHW041854070526
838199LV00045BB/1589